edexcel

Edexcel GCSE

History A: The Making of the Modern World

Unit 2C: The USA 1919–41

Author:
Jane Shuter

Series Editors:
Nigel Kelly
Angela Leonard

Updated for the
2013 specifications by:
Jane Shuter

ALWAYS LEARNING

PEARSON

Contents: delivering the Edexcel GCSE History A (The Making of the Modern World) specification Unit 2C

Welcome to the course

Welcome to Modern World History! Studying this subject will help you to understand the world you live in: the events of the last 100 years can help to explain the problems and opportunities that exist in the world today.

There are four units in the course and each is worth 25% of the whole GCSE. Those units are:

- Unit 1 International Relations: The era of the Cold War 1943–91
- Unit 2 Modern World Depth Study (Germany 1918–39; Russia 1914–39; or USA 1919–41)
- Unit 3 Modern World Source Enquiry (War and the transformation of British society c1903–28; War and the transformation of British society c1931–51; or The transformation of British society c1951–79)
- Unit 4 Representations of History (your controlled assessment task).

Introduction to Unit 2C

This book covers Unit 2C: The USA 1919–41. This is the 'Depth Study' section of your course, in which you study just one country, the USA, for just over 20 years. Focusing down on one country means you will be able to understand in more detail the changes in the USA between the end of the First World War and the start of the Second World War. First there was an economic boom – most people had well-paid jobs and their standard of living was getting better. Then there was a slump – millions lost their jobs, until the Americans elected a new President with new policies, which helped solve the crisis.

The exam for this section lasts 1 hour 15 minutes, and you must answer six questions. The questions test your knowledge of what happened, through your understanding of the causes and consequences of events, and the key features of what happened.

How to use this book

There are four key topics in this book and you have to study all of them for the exam.

- Key Topic 1: The US Economy 1919–29
- Key Topic 2: US Society 1919–29
- Key Topic 3: The USA in Depression 1929–33
- Key Topic 4: Roosevelt and the New Deal 1933–41

These key topics are the heart of this book. When you understand them, there is a further section in the book, examzone, to help you prepare for the exam.

Key terms are emboldened in the text, and definitions can be found in the glossary.

We've broken down the six stages of revision to ensure you are prepared every step of the way.

Zone in: how to get into the perfect 'zone' for revision.

Planning zone: tips and advice on how to plan revision effectively.

Know zone: the facts you need to know, memory tips and exam-style practice for every section.

Don't panic zone: last-minute revision tips.

Exam zone: what to expect on the exam paper.

Zone out: what happens after the exams.

These features help you to understand how to improve, with guidance on answering exam-style questions, tips on how to remember important concepts and how to avoid common pitfalls.

There are three different types of Examzone features throughout this book:

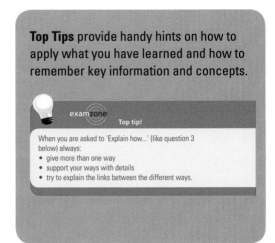

Top Tips provide handy hints on how to apply what you have learned and how to remember key information and concepts.

examzone
Top tip!

When you are asked to 'Explain how...' (like question 3 below) always:
- give more than one way
- support your ways with details
- try to explain the links between the different ways.

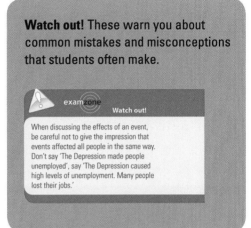

Watch out! These warn you about common mistakes and misconceptions that students often make.

examzone
Watch out!

When discussing the effects of an event, be careful not to give the impression that events affected all people in the same way. Don't say 'The Depression made people unemployed', say 'The Depression caused high levels of unemployment. Many people lost their jobs.'

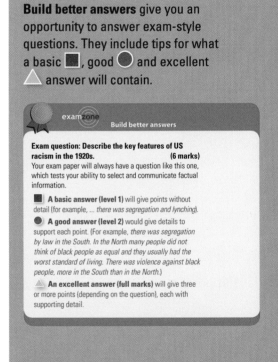

Build better answers give you an opportunity to answer exam-style questions. They include tips for what a basic ■, good ● and excellent ▲ answer will contain.

examzone
Build better answers

Exam question: Describe the key features of US racism in the 1920s. (6 marks)
Your exam paper will always have a question like this one, which tests your ability to select and communicate factual information.

■ **A basic answer (level 1)** will give points without detail (for example, ... there was segregation and lynching).

● **A good answer (level 2)** would give details to support each point. (For example, there was segregation by law in the South. In the North many people did not think of black people as equal and they usually had the worst standard of living. There was violence against black people, more in the South than in the North.)

▲ **An excellent answer (full marks)** will give three or more points (depending on the question), each with supporting detail.

The Know Zone Build better answers pages at the end of each section include an exam-style question with a student answer, comments and an improved answer so that you can see how to improve your own writing.

examzone
Build better answers

Question 1 (a):
Tip: Part (a) questions will ask you to make an inference from a source and provide evidence from the source to support it.
Let's look at an example. Look at Source A on page 14.
What can we learn from this source about the USA in the 1920s? (4 marks)

Student answer	Comments
This source tells me that they had more cars and bathtubs than any other people on earth.	This answer merely repeats information contained in the source, so it would be marked in the bottom level. A good answer needs an inference (a judgement which is not actually stated in the source).

Let's rewrite the answer with that additional detail. The inferences are in bold.

This source tells me that **in the 1920s the USA was a very rich country** because they had more goods, like cars and bathtubs, than any other nation.	There are two inferences, and the main one is supported by reference back to the source.

Key Topic 1: The US Economy 1919–29

When the First World War ended in 1918, the US economy, unlike those of Europe, was in a boom. During the war, the USA had lent money to its European allies. It had sold them food and war goods. Many, but not all, people in the USA enjoyed great prosperity. After the war, Europe was devastated. It still needed food and economic help from the USA, which provided these while not becoming involved in international politics.

The US boom continued after the war. New industries mass-produced consumer goods, such as cars and radios, which ordinary people could buy for the first time on hire-purchase schemes. Spending rose, boosting profits, production and employment. Ordinary people began to buy shares in these profitable companies. But this boom had underlying problems. It relied heavily on continued spending and rising production. What would happen when demand fell? Also, while the new industries boomed, older industries (such as the coal industry) declined. As soon as European farmers began producing their own food again, US farmers faced a drop in demand and prices began to fall.

In this Key Topic you will study:

- post-war problems
- problems in agriculture
- causes and consequences of the economic boom.

The US Government

The USA stands for the *United States of America*, a union of 50 different states. The powers of government are split between the individual states and the central government, called the **Federal** Government. The **Constitution**, drawn up when the original thirteen colonies rebelled against British rule, says which powers stay with the individual states, and which go to the Federal Government. You will not be asked about this in the exam, but you need to understand how the system works to understand what happened.

Federal
- Declare war
- Armed forces
- Foreign policy
- Regulate interstate trade
- The currency

Shared
- Law & order
- Taxes
- Court system
- Regulate banks
- Public welfare

State
- Education
- Local government
- Regulate trade within the state
- Marriage laws

Legislative (Congress)
- Passes laws
- Agrees taxes
- Agrees President's appointments of judges and ministers

Executive (President)
- Proposes laws
- Runs foreign policy
- Appoints government ministers
- Commands armed forces

Judicial (Supreme Court)
- Interprets constitution and laws
- Final appeal court

President
- Checks Congress because can veto laws.
- Checks Supreme Court because President appoints judges.

Congress
- Checks President's power because can reject appointments or overturn the President's veto, and can withhold taxes.
- Checks Supreme Court because can pass new laws and change the constitution (if States agree)

Supreme Court
- Checks President because can say actions are unconstitutional.
- Checks Congress because can say actions are unconstitutional.

The top diagram shows how the main powers of government are split – some with the states, some with the Federal Government, and some shared.

The Constitution split the Federal Government into three parts. This is called *the separation of powers*. The aim was to stop any one part becoming so powerful it could take freedom away from the people.

- The **legislative** branch that passes the laws is called **Congress**. It has two elected houses, the House of Representatives and the Senate.
- The **executive** branch, headed by the President, runs the government.
- The **judicial** branch, the Supreme Court, has the power to overturn anything that is against the Constitution or the law.

These two diagrams show how the main powers were divided between the three parts of the Federal Government, and how each part acted as a check to stop the other two parts getting too powerful.

Activities

1. Draw your own diagram to show the powers of the President, and the limits on the President's power.

2. Are there people or institutions with the same powers as the President, Congress, and the Supreme Court in Britain today?

Impact of the First World War

> ## Learning objectives
>
> In this chapter you will learn about:
> - how the war boosted industry and agriculture
> - the effect of Europe's post-war needs
> - key features of post-war isolationism.

Europe at the end of the war

When the First World War ended in 1918, the economies of most European countries were in ruins. Some had borrowed huge sums of money from the USA to finance the war. Trade links and production of ordinary goods had been disrupted by the war. In many countries mines, factories and communication links had been destroyed by the fighting. Britain and France were heavily in debt to the USA, and still borrowing – they needed more money to rebuild and start normal life again. Britain's wartime and post-war borrowings added up to a total of $4,277 million; while France owed $3,405 million.

The USA at the end of the war

The USA had no war damage. Just the opposite. Its factories and farms were producing goods and food at full capacity. It was exporting food and all sorts of manufactured goods to Europe, and it had won new export markets that, before the war, the Europeans had dominated, such as supplying cotton to Japan. The war gave the USA high productivity and full employment, with good wages for its workers.

Industry

Many industries began to apply the principles of **mass production** during the war, making their factories more efficient. When the war ended, they were in a good position to produce goods quickly and cheaply, both for the home market and for exports.

Year	Wheat ($ per bushel)
1915	$0.96
1917	$2.04
1919	$2.16
1921	$1.01
1923	$0.92

Source A: *Price of wheat from farming statistics compiled by the US government.*

US international loans (in $ millions)			
	Wartime loans	Postwar loans	Total loans
To the countries who were allies in First World War	$7,067m	$2,911m	$9,977m

Source B: *From US government figures.*

Activity

Begin to compile a graph of the price of wheat in dollars per bushel. Draw a graph where one axis runs from 1915 to 1945 and the other runs from $0 to $2.5, with each dollar divided into ten segments. Plot the prices from Source A onto the graph. You will add to the graph as you go through the book.

Agriculture

America's European allies suffered terrible food shortages in the last years of the war. Campaigns like Source D aimed to reduce US consumption, leaving more food to sell to Europe. Farmers played their part too. They expanded their farms, often taking out loans to buy new land and machinery. They also ploughed up land previously used for grazing cattle and sheep and grew wheat instead. Prices rose so high during the war that farmers were confident that they would sell crops at a good profit and repay their loans. In the early 1920s, the USA was producing 30% of the world's wheat, 75% of its corn and 55% of its cotton. It produced 70% of its petrol, too. It saw itself as the world's banker and the world's supplier of necessities.

A time of adjustment

The government, meanwhile, believed in **laissez faire**: letting businesses run their own affairs rather than passing laws to control working hours, prices or wages. *Laissez faire* led to problems immediately after the war, when the prices of crops fell and many employers reduced wages. There was discontent, strikes and people lost their jobs. Those who still had jobs found that their hours of work were reduced. But the government felt that all this was part of the economy returning to normal after its huge wartime push. It hoped that falling prices would eventually even things out without government interference.

Coolidge [President 1923–29] believed in as little government interference as possible and declared, 'the business of America is business'. Very soon, America was revelling in what became known as 'Coolidge prosperity'. It had very little to do with him and everything to do with the fact that America, after the First World War, was the country the world owed money to. Its undamaged industries achieved miracles of production on the first great assembly lines. It had the highest average income of any country. It made more steel than Europe. And Henry Ford built a car that almost everyone could afford.

Source C: *from* America, *written by Alistair Cooke in 1976.*

This is
what GOD gives us
What are you giving
so that others may
live?

Eat less
WHEAT
MEAT
FATS
SUGAR

Send more to Europe
or they will Starve

UNITED   STATES   FOOD   ADMINISTRATION

Source D: *A US government poster produced in 1918.*

examzone
Build better answers

What can you learn from Source C about prosperity in the USA? **(4 marks)**

This is an *inference* question. It asks you to work something out from the source.

■ **A basic answer (level 1)** will give information from the source (for example, *it was called Coolidge prosperity*).

● **A good answer (level 2)** will make an inference (for example, *that it was prosperous and had the strongest industry in the world*) without supporting it from the source.

▲ **An excellent answer (level 3)** will use details from the source to support the inference (for example, by adding *because it was undamaged by the war, had plenty of raw materials like steel, and was the first to use mass production*).

Isolationism

While the USA was willing to be the world's banker after the war, it was less happy to become involved in world politics. Woodrow Wilson [President 1913–21] played a major part in negotiating the treaties that ended the war and urged the setting up of the League of Nations. On his return to the USA, he found that many Americans, and most of the US Senate, did not want to join the League, or to be involved in world affairs at all. Instead, they wanted a policy of **isolationism** – not becoming involved in world politics. Their first isolationist step was to refuse to join the League of Nations.

Financial isolationism

The government still had a policy of *laissez faire* – not interfering in business. However, it made some exceptions in the early 1920s to make the USA's economic independence more secure. It introduced laws to keep the government 'living within its budget' and lowered the high wartime taxes. It also introduced trade tariffs – taxes on goods imported into the USA. This pushed up the price of imports, encouraging Americans to 'buy American'.

- **May 1921, Emergency Tariff Act:** increased the import taxes on wheat, sugar, meat, wool and other agricultural products.
- **June 1921, Budget and Accounting Act:** put controls on government spending.
- **November 1921, Revenue Act:** changed taxes, charging businesses more, but cutting the wartime tax on high levels of profit.
- **September 1922, Fordney and McCumber Tariff Act:** raised tariffs and extended them to industrial goods. It also gave the president the power to raise the tariff yearly, in line with the selling price of these goods in the USA.

These tariffs did encourage Americans to buy American goods. However, they did not help US exports. Other countries retaliated by introducing tariffs of their own, so US exports became more expensive and so less popular.

Activities

1 What can you learn about the USA in the 1920s from:
   a Source E?
   b Source F?
   c Source G?

2 Describe the USA's move to isolationism in the 1920s.

3 Explain the effects of the First World War on the economy of the USA.

How shall you keep from meddling in the affairs of Europe or keep Europe from meddling in the affairs of America? I will not, I cannot, give up my belief that America must, not just for the happiness of her own people, but for the moral guidance and greater contentment of the world, be permitted to live her own life.

Source E: *From a speech by William E Borah in the Senate on 19 November 1919. He was urging the Senate to vote against joining the League of Nations.*

Tariffs did nothing to foster co-operation among nations. They quickly became a symbol of the 'beggar-thy-neighbour' policies, adopted by many countries during this time, which contributed to a drastic reduction of international trade once they had taken effect. For example, US imports from Europe declined from a 1929 high of $1,334 million to just $390 million in 1932, while US exports to Europe fell from $2,341 million in 1929 to $784 million in 1932. Overall, world trade declined by some 66% between 1929 and 1934.

Source F: *From a discussion of protectionism on a US government history website in 2009.*

examzone
Top tip!

Good answers to 'Describe' questions (like 2 above) usually make several points, and support each point with some detail taken from the course.

Immigration restrictions

Another feature of US isolationism was its introduction of restrictions on **immigration**. Previously, it had had an 'open-door' policy, allowing unlimited immigration – although there were growing demands for restrictions on this. From 1900 to 1920, 12.5m Europeans had **emigrated** to the USA (many were unskilled workers from Italy and Eastern Europe) as had 1.5m from Canada, Asia and Mexico. This high figure was despite the fact that for several years the war had reduced emigration to a trickle.

As part of the government's isolationist drive to 'keep America American', it passed laws to cut immigration sharply. The law set the limits based on US census details of immigrants already in the USA, and aimed to make the greatest cut in numbers from Eastern Europe and Italy. There was a high level of prejudice in the USA against these immigrants who were wrongly seen as stupid, inferior and more likely to commit crimes. The 1921 Emergency Quota Act restricted immigration to 3% of the number of immigrants in the USA in 1910 (taken from the census) from any country. The 1924 Immigration Act reduced this to 2% and set a limit of 150,000 a year.

American institutions rely on good citizenship. New arrivals should be limited to our capacity to absorb them into the ranks of good citizenship. America must be kept American. For this purpose, it is necessary to continue a policy of restricted immigration. I am convinced our present economic and social conditions warrant a limitation of those to be admitted.

Source G: *Part of a speech made by President Calvin Coolidge to Congress on 6 December 1923.*

Source H: *A cartoon published in a US newspaper on 19 May 1921.*

Did you know?

Fear of communism played a key part in US restrictions on eastern European immigrants in the 1920s. This fear, known as the 'Red Scare', drove the Palmer Raids of New Year's Day 1920 in which over 6000 suspected communists were imprisoned. Many were released soon after, yet there was little outcry at the illegality of the raids. In fact, at the time, anarchists and communists only made up perhaps 0.1% of America's population.

Mass production

> ### Learning objectives
>
> In this chapter you will learn about:
> - key features of mass production
> - effects of mass production
> - the importance of the Ford motor industry.

Mass production was one of the important factors behind the economic boom. Mass production meant goods could be made more quickly and more cheaply. The pioneer of mass production was Henry Ford, who applied the system to car manufacture just before the war.

Mass producing a Ford

This is how the Ford motor works applied the principles of mass production.

- They made just one kind of car, so the parts were a standard size and shape. This saved on money, storage and time. **Standardisation** also saved on labour, as workers only had to learn how to deal with one set of parts.
- They introduced **division of labour**. Instead of one or two workers building a whole car, the work was split up into a series of jobs, with one worker doing the same job over and over on lots of cars. They found splitting up the jobs into lots of steps made assembly faster.
- In 1914, they introduced a moving **assembly line**. Each worker stayed in one place and the job came to them on a moving line. Using an assembly line and breaking the jobs into smaller steps to suit the line meant that the time taken to produce a car dropped from 12 hours to 1 hour and 33 minutes.

Not just cars

Once Ford had shown how effective mass production was, many other businesses began to apply mass-production methods in their factories. The assembly-line system was especially suitable for newer industries that produced finished goods such as radios and fridges.

In April 1913, we experimented with an assembly line, just on the magneto. We try everything in a little way first – we'll rip out anything once we find a better way, but we must be certain the new way will be better before doing anything drastic.

One workman could make one magneto in 20 minutes. Dividing his job into 29 steps cut the assembly time to 13 minutes, 10 seconds. Then we raised the height of the line 8 inches. This cut the time to 7 minutes. Changing the speed of the line cut the time down to 5 minutes.

Source A: From My Life and Work, Henry Ford's autobiography, first published in 1922.

Did you know?

Ford began by experimenting with a number of different models of car. In 1909, he decided to manufacture just one design, the Model T, and to make it in just one colour – black. This was because black paint was the quickest to dry.

The Model T led to the weaving of the first highways, then freeways and the interstate. Beginning in the early 1920s, people who had never taken a holiday beyond the nearest lake or mountain could explore the whole United States. Most of all, the Model T gave to the farmer and rancher, miles from anywhere, a new pair of legs.

Source B: From America, written by Alistair Cooke in 1976.

The effects of mass production

Mass production made goods cheaper, because they could be produced faster and so for less cost. But it had far more widespread effects, too. Consider again the example of Ford cars. In 1908 a Ford car, produced with standard parts and some labour specialisation, cost around $850. In 1926, an improved version of the car cost $300. This goes some way to explaining why there were 1m cars in the USA in 1915, but 28m in 1939.

Factories employed more people to make cars and car parts. Ford dealerships not only sold cars, they also provided mechanics to look after the cars and replace parts that wore out or were faulty. By 1912, there were 7,000 Ford dealerships in the USA and they spread rapidly. As the number of cars in the USA grew, so did the number of garages providing petrol and mechanics, all providing jobs. By 1929, over 4 million workers depended on the car industry. Industries that provided raw materials for parts (glass, steel, rubber and leather) also grew. By 1929, 75% of all leather, glass and rubber went to the car industry. The demand for petrol and oil grew, too.

More employment meant that more people had money to spend, which boosted industry. The growth in the number of cars led to more garages and surfaced roads (about 400,000km were built in the 1920s). Road travel became quicker and easier. So people travelled more often, spreading their spending. Travelling salesmen took to the road too, selling everything from vacuum cleaners to underwear.

Activities

1 Explain the effects of:
   a Experimentation on the development of mass production by Ford.
   b Mass production on the cost of a Model T Ford.
   c The fall in the price of cars on sales of Ford cars.

2 How does Source C show the effects of mass production? Make a list, explaining each effect fully.

3 Draw a diagram to show the effect of mass production of cars on the US economy. The diagram on page 15 may help you.

Source C: *A garage in Atlanta, Georgia, photographed in 1936 as part of a government photographic survey of living conditions all over the USA.*

Boom!

Learning objectives

In this chapter you will learn about:
- how new industries grew
- the effects of hire purchase
- the influence of advertising.

At the end of the war, the new industries that had been growing slowly before the war suddenly exploded into life. It seemed as if everyone was buying radios, cars, fridges, washing machines and telephones. What set off this sudden outbreak?

Reasons to buy

There were several reasons for the increase in demand for these new goods. Mass production made them cheaper. Prices of radios, cars, fridges and other goods were falling all through the 1920s. But mass production was not the only factor. Wages were rising – the average wage rose 8% in the 1920s. Many of these goods ran on electricity, and after the war many more homes were connected to the electric grid. Advertising became big business in the 1920s, creating demand by persuading people they wanted and needed a fridge or a car.

Perhaps the biggest factor of all in the growth of these new industries was **hire purchase**. The fact was that many people could not afford to buy the new luxury goods outright. So shops and businesses set up payment-in-instalments schemes to get over that difficulty. Customers signed a hire-purchase agreement and put down a deposit on a radio or car. They then took the goods and paid off the rest of the cost in regular instalments. Before the war, some businesses had offered schemes like this. But they were seen as not quite respectable – a way of paying that poor people had to use because they could not buy even their necessities outright. After the war, more and more people made purchases this way. Many people took out mortgages on their homes, too. Being in debt was no longer shameful.

When Hoover took the oath as President in March 1929, he was proud and confident. 'We are a happy people – the statistics prove it. We have more cars, more bathtubs, oil furnaces, silk stockings and bank accounts than any other people on earth.'

Source A: *From* The Free and the Unfree. A New History of the United States, *written by Peter N Carroll and David W Nobel in 1988.*

Year	Fridges made	Radios made
1921	5,000	No record
1923	18,000	190,000
1925	75,000	2,350,000
1927	390,000	1,980,000
1929	890,000	4,980,000

Value of goods produced in millions of dollars			
Year	Radios	Electrical goods	Toys and sporting goods
1921	12.2	63.2	124.1
1923	50.3	76.3	167.1
1925	168.2	106.3	164.2
1927	181.5	146.3	182.5
1929	366.0	176.7	214.6

Source B: *Some statistics that show the growth in production of consumer goods.*

examzone

Watch out!

When asked to explain why something happened, do not just give a general description of the event. Give an explanation with examples you can remember from studying the course.

The boom cycle

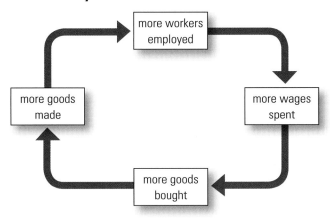

Source C: An advertisement for a fridge from 1931. Unlike many adverts, it actually does mention hire purchase ('a few dollars down places one in your home today!'). This may well be because General Electric, the manufacturers, had their own hire-purchase schemes.

Activities

1 Turn the 'reasons to buy' paragraph into a list of bullet point headings.

2 Re-draw the 'boom' diagram, inserting: 'higher demand for goods', 'more profits' and 'more demand for goods' in the right places on the cycle.

3 In pairs, using the Build better answers box, write a level 1 answer, a level 2 answer and a level 3 answer to this question:

Explain why people were buying so many more consumer goods in the 1920s.

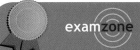

examzone
Build better answers

Exam question: Explain why hire purchase was important to the growth of the US economy.   (8 marks)

The examination will always have questions on *why things happened* – like this one.

■ **A basic answer (level 1)** would give one or two reasons why hire purchase was important, without any information to support them.

● **A good answer (level 2)** would give detailed information to illustrate each reason (for example, *... so people could buy goods that they would not have been able to pay for all at once. They made a down payment then paid a small sum at regular intervals.*).

▲ **A better answer (level 3)** would explain how each reason was linked to the outcome (for example, *... and if people bought things they wouldn't otherwise have been able to afford, the factories sold more of those goods than they would have done without hire purchase.*).

▲ **An excellent answer (full marks)** would show links between reasons (for example, *Factories could make more goods, knowing people could buy on hire purchase, and if demand went up then they could expand their factories and hire more people who would buy more goods. It all depended on people keeping on buying, and hire purchase encouraged that.*).

Buying shares

The confidence that came with the boom cycle and boosted it, led to a new development – ordinary people began to buy and sell **shares**.

What are shares?

Shares are just that, a 'share' in a company. If a person needs money to set up a company, or money to expand an existing company, the owner can raise that money by selling shares in the company. When the owner does this, he or she no longer owns all the company – the shareholders, the people who buy the shares, do. What they get in return for their shares is a yearly **dividend**. Each year, if it has made a profit, that profit is divided up between the shareholders. The amount they get is calculated according to the number of shares they have. Before the 1920s, only wealthy people or banks bought shares. They bought shares in companies they thought would be successful and would pay a good dividend, and they usually kept the shares for a long time. If shareholders needed money, they could sell their shares. Shares were not sold from person to person. For most companies they could only be bought and sold at a stock exchange – the most important was the New York Stock Exchange in Wall Street.

How the stock market worked

The **stock market** is the general name for buying and selling shares. Shares had no set value. They were worth whatever someone was prepared to pay for them. If you bought a share in a company for $10 one week, it could be worth $10 the next week, or $100 or $1. It all depended on the demand for the shares. The people who traded shares were called 'brokers'. If trading was 'slow', the prices of shares could stay the same for days, weeks or months. But, if there was a lot of buying and selling in the stock market prices could go up and down several times a day.

In the 1920s, because new companies made such big profits, the prices of their shares went up and up. More and more people bought shares. People started to buy shares not for the dividend, but to sell them again at a profit.

In 1929, Samuel Crowther interviewed John J Raskob [from the finance section of General Motors] about how an ordinary person could get rich by investing in stocks. Crowther published Raskob's ideas in a *Ladies' Home Journal* article, 'Everybody Ought to be Rich'. In the interview, Raskob claimed that putting just $15 a month into shares would make investors $80,000 over the next 20 years. The prospect of building such a great fortune seemed possible in the atmosphere of the 1920s market. Shares excited investors; millions put their savings into the market hoping for a quick profit.

Source D: *From* Stocks for the Long Run, *written by Jeremy J Siegel in 2008.*

Year	$ millions spent on share trading
1926	450.8
1927	576.6
1928	919.7
1929	1,125.0
1929	890,000

Source E: *From* A History of the Federal Reserve, *written by Allan Meltzer and Alan Greenspan in 2003.*

Company	3 March 1928	3 Sept 1929
Woolworths	$1.81	$2.51
Radio	$0.94	$5.05
AT & T (telephone company)	$0.77	$3.04
Westinghouse (electrical goods)	$0.92	$2.89
General Motors (cars)	$1.40	$1.82

Source F: *The price of a share in selected companies in 1928 and 1929.*

The stock market boom

As more and more people began buying shares, demand for shares, especially in new industries such as radios or electrical appliances, went up sharply. Because more people wanted to buy shares, the prices of shares rose and kept rising. From 1927, it seemed that everyone was buying shares and no one could lose.

Buying on the margin

People became so confident that the price of shares would keep going up that they began to borrow money to buy shares, confident that they would be able to sell them for more and repay the loan. Banks began to use their money to buy shares. They were gambling with people's savings. By autumn 1929, even the banks were beginning to forget that the price of stocks could go down as well as up.

Activities

1 Turn the 'What are shares?' paragraph into a flow diagram like the one on this page. Begin with someone wanting money to start a business.

2 Turn the 'How the stock market worked' paragraph into a similar flow diagram.

3 **a** If you had bought $30 worth of shares in radio and $30 worth of shares in AT & T on 3 March 1928, what would they be worth on 3 September 1929?

 b If you wanted to keep making money, what would you do with the profits?

4 In pairs, read the following question and write a level 1 answer, a level 3 answer and a level 2 answer to it.

Explain why people were buying so many more consumer goods in the 1920s.

How people hoped to get rich by 'buying on the margin'.

Not all winners

Learning objectives

In this chapter you will learn about:

● people who did not share the prosperity

● industries that did not boom

● reasons for the problems.

Year	Wheat ($ per bushel)		
1919	$2.16	1925	$1.44
1921	$1.01	1929	$1.04
1923	$0.92		

Source A: *From US government records of wheat prices in the USA. Prices are in dollars per bushel.*

Not everyone shared in the boom of the 1920s. Some older industries suffered after the war. Farmers had problems too – and about 40% of all workers were farmers and farm workers. Other people who suffered were black people and poor immigrants, many of whom could not afford food, let alone radios or cars.

The older industries

Older industries such as coalmining, shipbuilding and the railways could not benefit from new ideas such as the assembly line. During the war, these industries were at full production. After the war, the use of coal dropped rapidly. More people used cheaper electricity for heat, light and cooking. Businesses switched to electric power, too. The railways lost custom as people bought cars and many businesses chose instead to transport goods by truck on the network of surfaced roads that spread across the country. The war had increased the need for new ships, but demand had fallen now.

Problems for farmers

During the war, farmers bought more land (often by borrowing money on a mortgage), and they bought farm machinery (again, with borrowed money) to grow more food. They were growing for the European market as well as the home market. After the war ended, European farm production slowly recovered and then Europe needed much less food from the USA. Demand fell for other reasons too:

● in 1920, **Prohibition** (a ban on alcohol) reduced demand for grapes and barley (used to make wine and beer)

● many clothes were made from new, synthetic, fabrics such as rayon: demand for cotton and wool fell. This also had a knock-on effect in the traditional textile industry.

Farmers' costs were high, and prices were falling. Mechanisation meant they needed fewer workers, but they were growing more crops than the country needed. Prices fell, and farmers started to go bankrupt.

Build better answers

Was the development of new technologies the main reason why farming and the older industries did not share the prosperity of the boom years? Explain your answer. You may use the following in your answer:

● **war production**

● **competition in new industries.**

You must also include information of your own.

(16 marks)

■ **A basic answer (level 1)** makes a simple generalisation about causes.

● **A good answer (level 2)** agrees and/or disagrees with the proposition but does not explain how other causes offered were causes (for example … *the railways were in trouble because more people were using cars and the coal industry because of electricity.* A more complete answer will examine more than two causes.

▲ **A better answer (level 3)** will explain the causes discussed (for example, … *The coal industry was declining because of electricity which was a new industry producing a cheaper, cleaner, fuel .*

▲ **An excellent answer (level 4)** will prioritise the causes, or see links between them (for example, … *the new industries were probably the main reason, because they affected several older industries (coal production declined as electricity was used more; as more people bought cars, they travelled on trains less). But farming was affected by factors unrelated to new industries: such as over-producing despite European farmers growing more food and Prohibition causing a drop in demand for wine and beer ingredients.*

This question has up to 4 extra marks for spelling, punctuation and grammar.

Did you know?

Sharecropping replaced slave-labour on farms in the South after the Civil War. Instead of receiving a wage, the workers were paid a share of the crop they harvested, leaving them hit hard by low prices. Sharecroppers were the single most deprived group in the US in the 1920s.

Exam-style question

Describe the problems faced by some parts of the US economy in the early 1920s.   (6 marks)

Low paid workers

The other people who suffered during the boom were low paid workers and **sharecroppers.** These included farm labourers (many of whom were black) and workers in the worst-paid industries, as well as those who could find no work. Workers in the South were often paid less than those in the North. Wages varied all over the country. The average wage for a farm worker in 1919 was $13.5 a week. In 1925, it was $11.3 and by 1930 it had dropped to $7.5. And while some farm workers will have earned more than this, others will have earned less. Meanwhile the average teacher's wage had risen from $15.5 in 1919 to $29.9 in 1930, and a skilled factory worker's wage had gone from $22.3 to $28.6.

Activities

1   Add the prices in Source A to the graph you began for Question 1 on page 8.

2   Read the following answers to the question in the Build better answers box. Decide what level each answer should have.

Answer 1 Not really, it was a reason, but there were many other connected reasons that all contributed to the problems that farming and the older industries had.

Answer 2 The coal industry mostly declined because people were switching to electricity and the railways because people were switching to cars. The decline is tied to the new industries, but it isn't to do with the new technologies so much.

Advertising

Learning objectives

In this chapter you will learn about:
- reasons behind the rise in consumerism
- the power of advertising.

Activities

1   In pairs, turn the advert for a Victrola (Source A) into a jingle for radio. Keep it short, but use the same ideas.

2   Was the reduction in working hours the main reason for the rise of consumerism?

    You may use the following information to help you with your answer.
- Working hours fell
- Wages increased
- Prices fell
- Advertising grew

The 1920s boom grew rapidly as a wave of consumerism swept the country. People bought more and more goods and spent more and more money on leisure. This was partly because they had more time and money. Working hours dropped after the war and most wages rose. At the same time, most prices fell. So people could buy more. New industries produced new goods for people to spend their money on.

The power of advertising

Advertising became big business. Adverts on billboards and in newspapers and magazines urged people to spend their money. They used pictures that showed a desirable lifestyle. The words they used tried to convince people that they needed the products in the advert. They also applied pressure by suggesting that by not buying these goods the consumer was in some way letting his family down. The idea of 'keeping up with the neighbours' had arrived.

Soon, advertising was everywhere: on billboards, in shop windows, painted on the sides of buildings. There were adverts on the radio, too. By 1925, 2,700,000 families had a radio, so it was a powerful tool for advertisers. Radio adverts had to be short – advertisers paid by the minute.

Did you know?

In 1922, the first radio advert was broadcast: by a radio company looking for advertisers. At first, radio adverts just described the product, then they used slogans. The first radio musical jingle was for Wheaties cereals, in 1926.

Source A: *A magazine advertisement for the latest in record players, from 1920.*

Underlying problems

Learning objectives

In this chapter you will learn about:

● the problems underlying the boom economy.

At the start of 1929, business was still booming in the USA. But some people were warning that there were problems ahead. Many people were moving from farms to the cities to find work, where there was not enough work for all the newcomers, despite the boom. Unemployment was rising.

Unemployment

Unemployment was also rising because large companies had put many smaller companies out of business and then cut their own workforce by more efficient use of mass-production techniques. They could produce more goods more quickly without employing as many people. Between 1926 and 1928 unemployment rose from 880,000 to 2,080,000.

Big business in control

Workers in the USA belonged to different **unions**, one or more for each major industry. The unions were in a poor position in the 1920s having been virtually driven out of business before the First World War. Businesses, not the government, set wages, hours of work and working conditions. During the war, unions had agreed not to strike. Now there was a series of strikes for better conditions. They failed. Too many workers feared unemployment to stand up to the employers for long. Some businesses began to lower wages and even refused to employ union members. So membership of the unions fell.

The government knew unemployment was rising and wages were falling. It saw businesses exploiting workers and working for their own profit rather than the good of the economy as a whole. It did nothing, as it still believed in *laissez faire*.

A new president

There was a presidential election in 1928, in which Coolidge decided not to run for re-election. The Republicans stressed how much they had done for the USA already. Their candidate, Herbert Hoover, won and became president in March 1929.

By 1928, it was clear to bankers and other financial experts that 'the Coolidge Prosperity' had passed its peak. The country was now in a slow decline. In spite of this, the American public were still being fed on stories of bold business enterprises and sudden wealth.

Source A: *From* Boom and Slump in Inter-War America, *written by Tony Triggs in 1987.*

Source B: *A cartoon about the problems of mass production, printed in a union magazine in 1927.*

Activity

Write the following on four small cards: *no government control of business* (laissez faire)*; companies can set their own wages; companies can set their own prices; big companies control most of the market.* On each card, write at least one problem that this economic situation could cause and how it could cause it.

During the summer of 1929, there were even more signs that the economy was in trouble.

Overproduction

The consumer boom was slowing. As unemployment rose and wages fell, so the demand for goods began to fall too. Most businesses were slow to notice this change. They had come to expect consumer demand to keep risin, so they kept producing goods. They overproduced and their warehouses filled with goods that they found harder and harder to sell.

Farmers had been overproducing some foods since the end of the war and the price of wheat had been falling since 1919. Now the price of other foods, such as sugar and coffee, also fell, and kept falling. The tariff system (see page 10) made the prices of raw goods from the USA, such as copper, cotton and wool, unattractive to overseas buyers. So demand fell and some producers were slow to catch up with the drop. Cotton and wool sales were hit by tariffs and also the production of new, synthetic, fibres. By the summer of 1929 prices for all these raw goods and foodstuffs were falling. People had so much stock that they were forced to sell it cheaply.

Borrowing

Banks had a huge problem when it came to lending money to their customers. They had lent businesses money to expand. They had lent consumers money to buy homes and consumer goods. They had lent people money to buy shares. They had also lent money to other countries, especially in Europe. During the boom, most people, businesses and other countries had made their repayments regularly. Now, all these groups faced financial difficulties. Other countries had their own economic difficulties. They did not want to repay bank loans; they wanted to borrow more. As sales and prices fell, businesses found it harder to keep up their repayments. Meanwhile, consumers found it harder to keep up repayments to businesses and banks as wages fell or unemployment struck.

> As prices steadily declined in the 1920s, farmers simply produced more crops to make the money they needed to cover their costs, and the result was greater surpluses at lower prices.

Source C: *From* Historical Dictionary of the Great Depression, *written by James Olsen in 2001.*

Source D: *A newspaper advertisement for Herbert C Hoover, issued during the presidential election campaign of 1928.*

Banks needed their loans repaid. They had bought shares with their investors' money, relying on the stock market boom to provide returns for these investors. As the economic situation worsened, some experts warned that the boom could not continue. Yet the banks still lent money to people to buy shares, who expected to sell them at a higher price, pay off their loan and make a profit. Both the banks and some ordinary people were just not aware of the worsening situation, or simply ignored the warnings. The boom years had encouraged over-confidence.

Activities

1 Turn the information from page 22 into a bulleted list of problems headed 'Long-term economic problems'.

2 Add the years from Source E to the graph of wheat prices you have been building up.

3 You are a farmer and your crop prices are falling. A friend has written to you asking what you are going to do about falling prices. Write back, explaining why your answer is to grow more crops.

Year	Wheat ($ per bushel)
1925	$1.44
1926	$1.22
1927	$1.19
1928	$1.00
1929	$1.04

Source E: *From farming statistics compiled by the US government. The price of wheat is shown in dollars per bushel.*

People were not concerned if their shares fell in value; most falls were followed by rapid rises. One reason for this was that falls attracted bargain-hunters, who guessed the price would soon recover. Their eager buying usually helped to bring this about.

Source F: *From* Boom and Slump in Inter-War America, *written by Tony Triggs in 1987.*

Underlying problems of the boom.

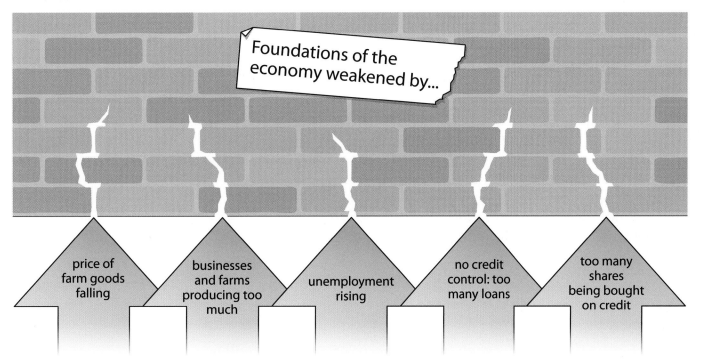

24 In the Unit 2 exam, you will have to answer six questions: Question 1 parts (a), (b), (c) and (d), and then one of 2(a) or 2(b) and one of 3(a) or 3(b).

You only have an hour and 15 minutes to answer these questions. Use the number of marks available for each question to help you judge how long to spend on each answer. Here we are going to look at questions 1(a) and 1(b). Allow about 6 minutes for 1(a) and 7 minutes for 1(b).

examzone

Build better answers

Question 1 (a):

Tip: Part (a) questions will ask you to make an inference from a source and provide evidence from the source to support it.

Let's look at an example. Look at Source A on page 14.

What can we learn from this source about the USA in the 1920s? (4 marks)

Student answer	Comments
This source tells me that they had more cars and bathtubs than any other people on earth.	This answer merely repeats information contained in the source, so it would be marked in the bottom level. A good answer needs an inference (a judgement which is not actually stated in the source).

Let's rewrite the answer with that additional detail. The inferences are in bold.

This source tells me that **in the 1920s the USA was a very rich country** because they had more goods, like cars and bathtubs, than any other nation.	There are two inferences, and the main one is supported by reference back to the source.

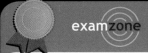
Question 1 (b):

Tip: Part (b) questions will ask you to explain the key features of an important event or policy. Sometimes the words 'key features' will actually appear in the question. Or you could be asked about problems, or policies or effects. Don't just tell the story. Think about the information and organise it as if you were putting it under headings. This type of question requires you to write at greater length than in part (a) and is worth 6 marks. Let's look at an example.

Describe the effects of mass production. (6 marks)

Student answer	Comments
The effects on the USA were that it became easier to make goods more cheaply.	This answer gives only one effect of mass production, and has added no detail.

Let's rewrite the answer with the detail added.

One effect was that it **became easier to make goods more cheaply**. With mass production the price of a car more than halved in the 1920s, **so more people could buy these cars**. This had the further effect of putting money back into the car industry so it could go on producing cars. Mass production created a demand for supplies **so industries that provided the raw materials for the mass- produced goods also benefitted (like the iron and steel industry for cars)**.	There are three developed effects here.

Key Topic 2:
US Society 1919–29

What was it like to live in the USA in the boom years of the 1920s? People had very different experiences, depending on their class, their sex, their occupation and their race. Some changes affected a large part of the population. The rise in consumerism, spurred on by the growth in advertising, was one of these factors. The movies had a huge impact, as did Prohibition – the government ban on alcohol introduced in 1920.

Something else that grew in the 1920s was organised crime. In some cities, gangs became more powerful than the mayor and local government. Along with gangsters and the atmosphere of violence they produced came groups such as the **Ku Klux Klan**, who took violent action against people they saw as 'un-American', including black people, communists and immigrants. Prejudice and discrimination were also evident in the supposedly fair legal system. For example, two men, Sacco and Vanzetti, political radicals from immigrant families, were tried and executed for robbery and murder (see page 38). The evidence was weak, and many people claimed they were really on trial for their ancestry and beliefs. Meanwhile, in the 'Monkey Trial' in Tennessee, a teacher was put on trial for teaching the theory of evolution.

In this Key Topic you will study:

- the roaring 20s
- Prohibition and gangsters
- racism and intolerance.

Consumerism

Spending money

The 1920s was the first decade of widespread consumerism. All people, of all ages and classes, were targeted by adverts. Everyone was urged to want something, to chase their dreams. While being in debt was seen as shameful, buying goods on hire purchase was respectable. If you believed the advertising, everyone did it. So homes filled with consumer goods and people drifted into debt.

Social impact of consumerism

Consumerism made people want, and buy, more goods. It also changed the way they lived and thought in other ways. In 1926 the National Broadcasting Company (NBC) set up the first national radio station and widespread ownership of radios (as well as the spread of movie theatres) gave people a national culture as well as a nationwide-centred view of things. People right across the country listened to the same radio shows and hummed the same popular tunes. Cars, and the increasing number of hard-surfaced roads, made travel easier. People travelled more often and further and were more likely to move for work.

Spending time

In the 1920s, people not only had more money to spend, they had more leisure time. They went out more – to movie theatres, sports stadiums and race tracks, recreation grounds and clubs. They ate out more, both in restaurants and in the cheap family diners that sprang up along the national highways. People also went on holiday more often. Their increasing leisure time made it possible and adverts encouraged people to get away by car, bus or train. This growth of leisure time led to a new, highly profitable, industry – the entertainment industry.

Source A: *By 1929, cars had moved a long way from Henry Ford's single design of car, painted black. Now cars came in many different colours and different styles targeted different consumers, from the sporty design aimed at the young man or woman out with a date to the bigger, more sedate 'family saloon'.*

That's entertainment!

> ### Learning objectives
>
> In this chapter you will learn about:
> - new forms of entertainment
> - reasons for the growth of the entertainment industry.

At home, people listened to the radio, but when they went out they were most likely to go to a sporting event or the movies. These were the entertainment industries that were the most profitable.

Sport

Radio coverage of sporting events, such as baseball or horse racing, increased their popularity and they were easier to reach thanks to better transport and more leisure time. Sports personalities became almost as famous as movie stars. The betting industry also boomed as people bet on their favourite horses or sporting teams. People also played more sport themselves. Golf courses and tennis courts sprang up everywhere and wealthy people set up their own golf and tennis clubs, where they could be sure only to mix with 'the right sort of people'.

The movies

Hollywood had been a centre for movie-making before the First World War. After the war, however, movie-making exploded. Early movies had no sound and some movie theatres hired a pianist to play suitable music to go with the screen action. Other movie theatres even hired orchestras. In 1922, cinemas made $4 million a week in ticket sales. People wanted homes, cars and clothes like the ones the movie stars had. The most famous stars, whose fans could make a movie a success, were highly paid. In 1916, Mary Pickford's weekly wage was $10,000 (the national average weekly wage was $13).

People wanted each new movie to be bigger and better than the last. Film directors hunted for the next star, the next 'big thing'. Then, in 1927, the 'talkies' arrived: films with a soundtrack so actors could speak. They caused chaos in the movie industry. Some film stars did not have good speaking voices (or their voices were not what their fans had imagined). Sound technology ruined John Gilbert's career. His first talkie had audiences roaring with laughter at his high voice – produced by poor technology. Other actors had difficulty learning lines and had to retire.

> The growing middle class, with larger paychecks and shorter working weeks, had the time and money to follow, even to play, sports. Radio broadcasts of football, boxing and horse racing, and newspaper sports columns boosted the popularity of spectator sports. Babe Ruth [baseball], Jack Dempsey [boxing] and Ruth Ederle [swimming] became national celebrities. Golf and tennis skyrocketed in popularity as men and women flooded to newly built golf courses and tennis courts.

Source A: *From* The 1920s, *written by Kathleen Morgan Drowne and Patrick Huber in 2004.*

> People living in the inner cities mostly went to local boxing halls, pool halls or bowling alleys to play sport. Once public transport became more affordable they could go to outlying ballparks and racetracks and watch sport.

Source B: *Leisure activities in the 1920s, described in* City Games, *written by Steven A Reiss in 1991.*

The Jazz Age

Jazz music had roots in black culture and spread throughout the USA as black people moved north across the country. In the 1920s it became a big craze, especially in nightclubs. Wild dances, such as the Charleston, were invented for the music and jazz came to symbolise the new, free age. The new record industry was soon selling jazz records for people to listen and dance to at home, even if they lived far from clubs.

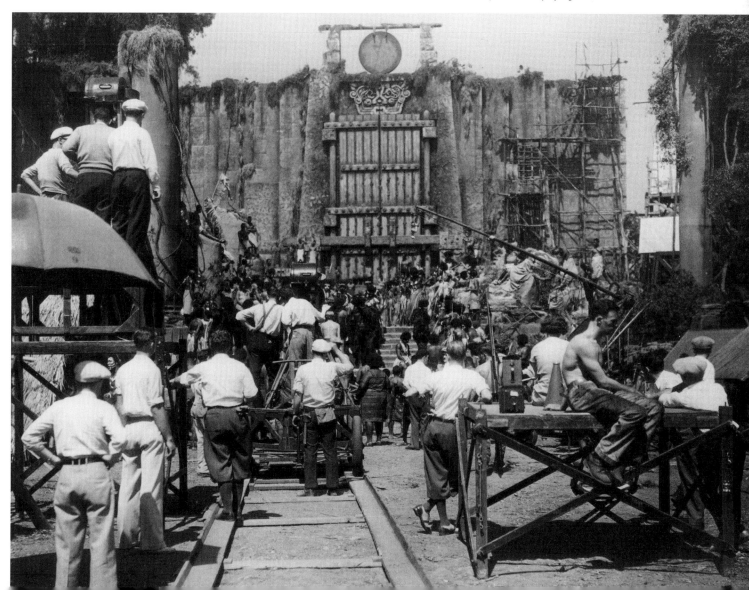

An immoral age?

Not everyone was swept away with the glamour of jazz and the movies. Some people thought they encouraged immorality. They thought jazz music, and the dances that went with it, were too sexual. They worried about the lifestyles shown in the movies. Women in the movies smoked and drank. Movies showed crimes being committed. Couples kissed on screen. Critics of the movies argued that this meant that people, especially women, eager to copy film stars would want to start smoking, drinking and kissing (and more) before marriage.

The wild lives of some film stars, reported in movie magazines and the newspapers, gave critics of the movies more ammunition. They said it was time for the movies to have a set of rules that limited what could be shown on screen. In 1930, the Hays Code was published. It set down rules for movies to make sure that, 'no picture shall be produced that will lower the moral standards of those who see it.'

Activities

1 What do Sources A and B tell you about how people used their leisure time in the 1920s?

2 What does Source C tell you about movie making in the 1930s?

3 In pairs, produce a list of four ways that people who criticised the movies and jazz music feared that they might 'lower the moral standards' of many people.

4 **a** List as many new jobs as you can that were created by the great success of the movies in the 1920s.

 b Explain the effects of the development of the movie industry on the economy. The diagram on page 15 may help you structure your answer.

Source C: *Filming the 1933 movie* King Kong. *The movie cost about $650,000 and made over $4m profit after paying off its costs.*

New women

Learning objectives

In this chapter you will learn about:

- how the role of women changed in the 1920s
- reasons for this change.

Exam-style question

What does Source C tell you about the position of women in the 1920s? (4 marks)

Effects of the war

Before the war, women in the USA were still struggling for **suffrage** (the right to vote). When the USA entered the war, the government asked women to do the work of men who had gone to war. Women went to work in their millions.

The war gave women the experience of independence, of earning wages and of showing what they were capable of doing. They had to work for lower wages than men, but even this was a victory. In 1918, even before the war was over, President Wilson urged the Senate to pass a federal law giving women equal voting rights, saying: 'We have made partners of the women in this war. Shall we allow them only a partnership of suffering and sacrifice and toil, and not a partnership of privilege and right?' The 19th Amendment to the United States Constitution, giving women equal suffrage, became law on 18 August 1920. After the war, women were expected to let the returning men have their jobs back. Most young women worked, but this was seen as only temporary, until they married.

	1910	1920	1930
White-collar workers			
Male	6,019	7,176	9,564
Female	1,943	3,353	4,756
Manual and service workers			
Male	13,469	16,172	18,956
Female	4,327	4,115	5,088
Farmworkers			
Male	10,359	10,221	9,414
Female	1,175	1,169	908
Total workers, male and female	37,292	42,206	48,686

Source B: *Men and women in the workforce, taken from US government statistics (in thousands).*

Activities

1 Use Source A to make a list of which states had full, partial and no voting rights in 1913. How many states had to make changes when women got the vote in 1920?

2 Use a spreadsheet or PowerPoint to find the best way to display the statistics in Source B.

3 In pairs, read the following answer to the question in the Build better answers box and decide what level it is.

There were flappers in the 1920s. They were very different from women before the war.

Now write a level 3 version of that answer.

Source A: *This 'Votes for Women' stamp from 1913, despite its positive message, shows that less than half the US states allowed women the vote on an equal level with men. The map shows states where women have 'partial suffrage' – some voting rights, but not equal to men.*

Flappers

'Flappers' was the name given to some young women in the 1920s. They did not depend on men to support them. They helped change western attitudes to women.

Flappers wore silk stockings and short dresses made from modern fabrics. They did not wear the traditional layers of underclothes or corsets, so their bodies were far more evident. They cut their hair short, in a 'bob'. They wore make-up and many of them smoked and drank. Most of them worked, alongside men (if not for equal pay). They went to racecourses, boxing matches and clubs. In short, they did things that previously only men had done. They did not conform to the image of women as home-based wives, mothers and daughters.

Many flappers married eventually. When they did, they had to change their behaviour. However, many of them took advantage of all the new household gadgets to live as labour-saving a home life as possible, and some even continued to work.

Source D: *One of the covers of a weekly magazine called* Judge *for the year 1925.*

Women were now competing with men in the business world more than ever before. Whereas before prohibition the saloon bar had been a male space, women now drank with men in speakeasies. Women had taken to swearing, smoking and using contraception. They were not keeping inside the limits of their traditional role. They were becoming financially, and therefore in other ways, independent of their fathers and husbands in record numbers.

Source C: *From an article on 'flappers', written in 1969.*

Prohibition and crime

> **Learning objectives**
>
> In this chapter you will learn about:
> ● effects of Prohibition
> ● reasons for the growth of the gangster culture.

Prohibition

Several groups (such as the Anti-Saloon League, set up in 1893) had been demanding an alcohol ban in the USA for a long time. They said drinking broke up homes and families and led to crime (some claimed it led to insanity, too). Employers complained that drinking made many workers unreliable. By 1917, alcohol was banned in several states, and during the war there was also a ban on brewing alcohol from grain, because the grain was needed for food. Congress passed the 18th Amendment to the Constitution, outlawing the manufacture, transport and sale of alcohol in December 1917, and it was **ratified** in January 1919, coming into effect in January 1920.

Millions of people still wanted to drink. It became clear that people would break this law if they could find a place to serve them. The '**speakeasy**' was born. Some speakeasies were like private clubs and served food as well as drink. They served 'bootleg' alcohol smuggled from other countries, such as Mexico. Others were simply bars, and alcohol was also sold in gambling dens. The worst places served 'moonshine' – home-brewed alcohol that could be very dangerous to drink.

Organised crime

Organised crime had existed in the USA for a long time. But Prohibition gave it the perfect conditions to grow. Gangsters took over the sale and distribution of alcohol, and since very many people wanted to drink, there were plenty of customers and plenty of profit. Gangsters ran gambling dens, fixed the betting at dog and horse races and ran brothels and clubs as well. Because they were making a great deal of money, they could often bribe the police, Prohibition Agents, judges, juries and local officials. Each gang controlled its own area and, inside that area, it was the law. Many businesses had to pay 'protection' money to the local gang, who would otherwise damage their business, or even destroy it.

A major underlying cause of the corruption in cities like Chicago was Prohibition. The corruption created by this unenforceable law became part of city life. Police and officials saw bribes as part of their income and the reporters who publicly scorned gangsters privately drank their illegal alcohol.

Source A: *From a biography of the gangster Al Capone, written in 1994.*

alcohol sales	$60m
gambling	$25m
brothels, dance halls	$10m
other illegal activities	$10m

Source B: *Profit made by Al Capone, a Chicago gang leader, in 1927 (from a biography of Capone written in 1930).*

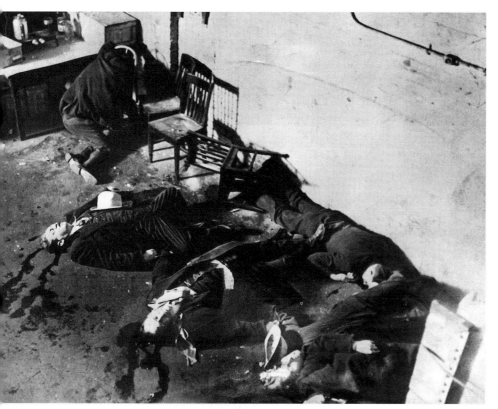

Source C: *The St Valentine's Day Massacre of 14 February 1929. Seven members of the Moran gang were trapped in a garage, lined up against the wall, and shot with sawn-off shotguns.*

Source D: *A cartoon called 'The King still reigns', published in 1930.*

Gang war

The powerful rival gangs fought each other for control of parts of cities such as Chicago. The most notorious example was on 14 February 1929, the St Valentine's Day Massacre, when Al Capone's gang killed seven members of the rival Bugs Moran gang in Chicago. No one was ever arrested. This was one of the more spectacular killings, but it was not unusual – that year there were about 400 gang-related killings in Chicago.

Many people blamed Prohibition for the gang violence. Prohibition gave the gangs money and power, and reduced respect for the law, because it involved millions of ordinary Americans in breaking the law. But there were other factors. The war had trained a generation of ex-soldiers, who were used to killing. Cars made it possible to make a surprise attack and a quick get-away. The fact that gangs made so much money meant that they could bribe politicians and the police. The fact that they were so violent meant that very few eyewitnesses were prepared to testify against them.

Did you know?

The word 'gangsterism' was used for the first time in the 1920s. It was used to mean behaving in a violent and lawless way.

Activity

1 a Why did the supporters of Prohibition want to ban alcohol?

   b Does this mean that Prohibition cannot have been a cause of the rise of organised crime?

2 Describe the way the United States Constitution is changed.

3 Explain how organised crime became so powerful in the USA in the 1920s.

4 Which of the sources in this unit is the best evidence of the power of organised crime in the 1920s?

Racism

> ### Learning objectives
>
> In this chapter you will learn about:
> - Jim Crow laws and racist attitudes
> - the Ku Klux Klan.

By 1870, the USA had abolished slavery and given black people equal rights as American citizens. In reality, however, black people still faced racism, unequal treatment and violence. All over the USA, black people often did the most unpleasant jobs and were 'last hired, first fired'.

Racism in the South

In the South, 'Jim Crow' laws enforced segregation – the policy of making black people use different, usually worse, facilities from whites. This covered everything from cafés to transport to toilets. States gave black schools less money, so it was hard to pay for books or building repairs. Black people had the right to vote, but white southerners often stopped them from registering to vote. Sometimes they told black people they would lose their jobs if they registered. Sometimes they threatened violence. The law in some states said voters had to be literate (able to read). So in those states, the (always white) person registering voters gave black people a hard test passage to read and white people a simple one. This 'legally' disqualified black people as illiterate.

Racism in the North

The North had no segregation laws, but black people often lived in separate neighbourhoods – usually in the worst parts of towns, so local schools and facilities were often all black anyway. But black people did have more opportunities to live a more equal life. They were more likely to get an education, and that education went on for longer. Many black people hoped that their contribution to the forces and war work during the war would help to change racism, especially in the South. It didn't, so many of them left. In the 1920s, black people moved north in their millions. In 1910, the black population of the Harlem area of New York was 10%. In 1920, it was 33% and by 1930 it was 70%.

Homer Plessy went to court to challenge a Louisiana railroad's forcing him to sit in a 'separate but equal' carriage, saying it was a violation of his rights under the constitution. Justice John Marshall Harlan said on his behalf: 'Our constitution is colour-blind'. The other justices did not agree; they ruled for the railroad. Separate but equal was legal. Jim Crow laws affected: public transport, shops, post offices, drinking fountains and libraries. Until the 1940s, the American Red Cross kept negro blood segregated in blood banks.

Source A: *From* Black History for Beginners, *written by Denise Dennis in 1984.*

Did you know?

'Jump Jim Crow' was a satirical caricature played by white actor Thomas D. Rice in the 1830s. The name came to be used as a derogatory term for African people, hence 'Jim Crow Laws'.

How white people in the North and South expected black people to behave.

Epilogue

I, too, sing America.

I am the darker brother.
They send me to eat in the kitchen
When company comes,
But I laugh,
And eat well,
And grow strong.

Tomorrow,
I'll sit at the table
When company comes.
Nobody'll dare
Say to me,
"Eat in the kitchen,"
Then.

Besides,
They'll see how beautiful I am
And be ashamed, –

I, too, am America

Source B: *From* The Weary Blues, *a collection of poems by the black poet Langston Hughes, written in 1926.*

Source C: *A segregated drinking fountain in the South. The 'colored' label has been nailed to the nearest tree. Legally, segregated facilities had to be clearly marked.*

Activities

1 Turn Source B into a letter to a newspaper, giving the same information and feelings.

2 In pairs, read the question and the answers below. Decide what level you would give the answers.

Explain how racism affected black people in the North differently from the South.

Answer 1: *It didn't affect them as much as the South but they still ended up with the worst deal.*

Answer 2: *It didn't affect them as much as the South, because there they had Jim Crow Laws that meant that if you didn't obey the segregation laws you could be put in prison.*

Exam question: Explain the effects of Jim Crow laws. (8 marks)

◼ **A basic answer (level 1)** will give one effect (for example, *black people had to live separately*) but no detail.

● **A good answer (level 2)** would give details about the effects. (For example, *Black people had to live separately by law, so they could go to prison if they used a drinking fountain for white people or the wrong carriage on a train.*)

▲ **A better answer (level 3)** would give at least two effects and explain how they came about.

▲ **An excellent answer (full marks)** would link them. For example: *They lived in segregated parts of town, usually the worst, bad housing and facilities so they probably got sick more, but then the hospitals were worse. In this way these laws affected their whole lives. The laws meant they were separated and their lives were really very unequal, because of the way one problem led to another.*

Racist violence

White racism was not just a matter of enforcing separation on black people. It was not even a matter of routinely treating them as inferior. There were racist groups who were quite happy to beat up, terrorise, or even murder black people for any reason or, sometimes, for no reason at all.

Lynch law

A lynching is when a mob kills somebody, because the people in the mob believe the person they lynch has committed a crime. In the USA in the early twentieth century it was usually (but not always), a white mob killing a black man. Sometimes the mob hauled their target from jail, sometimes the person had not even been arrested. Lynch mobs almost always beat or tortured their targets, then hanged their bodies from a tree. Many people at the time thought lynching only went on in the South. This was not true, but it was easier to get away with there.

Finally the mob attacked the massive jail, unfazed by a dozen tear gas canisters thrown by the sheriff and his deputies. Tom Shipp was beaten, stabbed, and lynched from the window bars on the east side of the jail. Abe Smith was clubbed, beaten and dragged to the Grant Courthouse Square. Smith was lynched in the square, after which some men returned to the jail, cut down Shipp's body, and carried it to the square to hang beside Smith's.

Source A: *Modern historian Dora Apel's description of the lynching by a mob of about 4000 people from her 2004 book,* Imagery of Lynching: Black Men, White Women, and the Mob.

Source B: *In 1930, Tom Shipp and Abe Smith were arrested on suspicion of murder in Indiana (not a southern state). Before they could be tried, they were taken from jail, beaten, then hanged by a mob of about 1,000 people.*

The Ku Klux Klan

The first **Ku Klux Klan** was a set up by a group of soldiers from the South in 1866, after they lost the Civil War. Its aim was to stop blacks gaining any real freedom. It was suppressed in the 1870s. In 1915, William Simmons re-formed the Ku Klux Klan. It was still a terrorist organisation, but it expanded its targets a little. The Klan wanted America to be a WASP nation (white Anglo-Saxon protestants). They saw black people, Jewish people, immigrants from non-Anglo Saxon countries, Catholics and people who belonged to left-wing political groups (for example Communists) as 'un-American'. They believed these people should be driven out of the country. The Klan became very powerful, especially in the South. They wore white robes and hoods, to keep their identity secret. In fact, almost everyone knew who was a local Klan member. In some states the police, the law courts and local government were all full of Klan members. It was hard for anyone they persecuted to bring charges against them.

Source C: *One of many songbooks produced for the Ku Klux Klan. 'Uncle Sam', the symbol of America, is carrying a US flag and leading a group of Klansmen.*

Activities

1 Write one or two sentences to explain what Source B tells you about the feelings of the lynch mob.

2 Why might people have hesitated to help Shipp and Smith?

3 In pairs, read the answers to the question below. Using the Build better answers box, say which is the better answer.

Explain the key features of the Ku Klux Klan.

a *It was a secret organization, whose members were White Anglo-Saxon Protestants. They wore uniforms with hoods to avoid being recognised, which intimidated blacks and other groups, often by lynching.*

b *They wore hoods and white uniforms and they were terrorists.*

 examzone

Watch out!

Many people make the mistake of calling the 'Ku Klux Klan' the 'Klu Klux Klan'. This is because the last two words both start with 'Kl-'. But the first word does not have an 'l' in it.

 examzone

Build better answers

Exam question: Describe the key features of US racism in the 1920s. **(6 marks)**

Your exam paper will always have a question like this one, which tests your ability to select and communicate factual information.

■ **A basic answer (level 1)** will give points without detail (for example, ... *there was segregation and lynching*).

● **A good answer (level 2)** would give details to support each point. (For example, *there was segregation by law in the South. In the North many people did not think of black people as equal and they usually had the worst standard of living. There was violence against black people, more in the South than in the North.*)

▲ **An excellent answer (full marks)** will give three or more points (depending on the question), each with supporting detail.

Intolerance

Learning objectives

In this chapter you will learn about:

- attitudes to immigrants
- religious intolerance.

The quota system introduced to limit the number of immigrants into the USA (see page 11) didn't stop many people being prejudiced against immigrants. For many this turned into **xenophobia**. Some prejudiced reasons given for objecting to immigrants were:

- immigrants were often poor people
- they were often unskilled
- they lived in poor, high-crime areas and did not learn the language
- some brought undesirable influences from their home country (the Mafia in Italy and Italian immigrant involvement in gangsterism was an example regularly given)
- some had communist political ideas.

Source A: *demonstration in New York against the 'guilty' verdict against Sacco and Vanzetti.*

The Sacco and Vanzetti case

On 15 April 1920 two men were killed and $15,777 stolen in a robbery. On 5 May, two men were arrested picking up a car the police thought was used for the crime. These men, Nicola Sacco and Bartolomeo Vanzetti, were Italian immigrants and also anarchists – a political group that believed in the violent overthrow of governments. The car was similar to the one used in the robbery. They were carrying guns when arrested; one of these used bullets of the same type as used in the crime. Vanzetti had been convicted of armed robbery before and the police had a long list of 'eyewitnesses' who were prepared to identify Sacco and Vanzetti.

But Sacco and Vanzetti had a long list of 'eyewitnesses' to say that they were elsewhere, and investigation techniques were not good enough to identify the car or bullets exactly. Each side accused the other of persuading people to be 'eyewitnesses'. There was no clear evidence. However, the judge at the trial made it clear that he expected a 'guilty' verdict. He got one. There were appeals, petitions and protests, in the USA and abroad. The men were finally executed on 23 August 1927.

Source B: *A cartoon about the Scopes trial, published in a New York newspaper at the time.*

The 'Monkey Trial'

Many religious groups rejected the theory of **evolution**. A conservative politician, William Jennings Bryan, campaigned to ban any teaching of evolution in schools. Bryan and his supporters poked fun at the theory of evolution by suggesting it said we were related to monkeys. In 1925, the state of Tennessee passed a law that banned the teaching of anything that contradicted the Bible's Creation story.

John Scopes, a high-school biology teacher in Dayton, Tennessee, deliberately taught evolution so there would be a court case to test whether the law was allowable under the Constitution. The trial caused a sensation. On the first day about 1,000 people crammed into the courtroom: 300 of them had to stand. The case was broadcast live on radio in Chicago. The defence said the state law was against the Constitution and should be overruled. The judge did not accept this argument. The defence then tried to call witnesses to test the idea of Creation in the Bible and the idea of evolution. The judge heard some evidence, then decided that this was irrelevant. He finally told the jury that the decision was simple. Was teaching against the Creation story illegal? Yes. Had Scopes done this? Yes. So he had broken the law. The jury found Scopes guilty and fined him $100. Despite appeals against the case, the Tennessee law was not repealed until 1967.

Activities

1   How did Sacco and Vanzetti fit the prejudices of some people against immigrants at the time?

2   What does Source A suggest to you about the Sacco and Vanzetti case?

3   Source B was in support of Scopes and against the law banning the teaching of evolution. Copy and complete this table, explaining how we know this.

Feature	Explanation
Teacher wears black glasses	Blind people wore black glasses, suggests teacher is made to wear dark glasses so he can't see the truth.

4   Either draw, or write a brief for an artist to draw, two cartoons:

   a   supporting the case against Sacco and Vanzetti, or supporting the ban on teaching evolution.

   b   against the trial and execution of Sacco and Vanzetti, or against the ban on teaching evolution.

   Use the information given in the text to bring out the ideas at the heart of the support and opposition to these two cases.

Know Zone
Unit 2C - Key Topic 2

In the Unit 2 exam, you will be required to answer questions on one country. You will have to answer six questions: Question 1 parts (a), (b), (c) and (d), and then one of 2(a) or 2(b) and one of 3(a) or 3(b).

You only have an hour and 15 minutes to answer these questions. Use the number of marks available for each question to help you judge how long to spend on each answer. Here we are going to look at questions 1(c) and 1(d). Allow about 10–12 minutes for each of them.

examzone
Build better answers

Question 1 (c):

Tip: Part (c) questions will ask you to use your knowledge of the topic to explain effects or consequences. There are 8 marks for this question and you are required to go into things in a little more depth than you have done on parts (a) and (b).

Explain the effects of Prohibition on US society in the 1920s. (8 marks)

Student answer	Comments
Prohibition was very bad for the USA because it led to the rise of gangsters like Al Capone. Gangsters made money from selling drink in illegal speakeasies and Capone controlled most of them in Chicago. He was responsible for the St Valentine's Day Massacre when 7 members of a rival gang were gunned down in a garage.	This answer is good about gangsterism, and the student has used accurate facts, like the seven men killed in the St Valentine's Day Massacre. However, it only talks about one effect, so it will be marked in level 2.
Prohibition was very bad for the USA because it led to the rise of gangsters like Al Capone **and corruption in politics**. Gangsters made their money from selling drink in illegal speakeasies and Capone controlled most of them in Chicago. He was responsible for the St Valentine's Day Massacre when seven members of a rival gang were gunned down in a garage. **The gangsters had so much money they could bribe prohibition agents, the police, and often local politicians. This corruption made all sorts of things in America worse, and ordinary people suffered because the politicians and the gangsters could do just what they liked.**	We now have a very good answer. It deals with more than one effect, and, in talking about how the profits of the gangsters were used to bribe the police and the politicians, it shows us the way the effects were linked together. This would get top marks.

Question 1 (d)

Tip: Part (d) questions will ask you to use your knowledge to explain why something happened. In other words, this is a question about causation. Let's look at an example.

Explain why Prohibition did not make the United States a better place to live in the 1920s. (8 marks)

Student answer	Comments
People still wanted to get a drink, so they broke the law. Gangsters made their fortune because they could make and sell the drink. The police and the mayors took bribes. Al Capone was probably responsible for over 400 murders.	The candidate knows all the problems and has explained them. Al Capone's responsibility for over 400 murders is a good supporting detail. As this is a cause explained using contextual knowledge, it would be marked in level 2. However, the candidate does not explain why these problems brought about the stated outcome (i.e. not making the United States a better place to live).

Let's rewrite the answer with the detail added.

It undermined the police and people's respect for the law. People still wanted to get a drink, so they broke the law. **This played into the hands of the** gangsters, who made their fortune because they could make and sell the drink. **The gangsters were breaking the law, but their business was profitable and they wanted to protect it. They fought other gangs and got** the police and the mayors to take bribes. Al Capone was probably responsible for over 400 murders. **Instead of being a place of less crime, as the people who supported Prohibition wanted, it made America a country with more crime, and very powerful criminals.**	Now we have the problems clearly linked to why things got worse, not better. It has clearly stated how the causes explained stopped America becoming a better place.

Key Topic 3: The USA in Depression 1929–33

In October 1929 the stock market boom ended with the Wall Street Crash. This led to a 'bust spiral' in the USA that was as extreme as its boom spiral had been. The US economy became caught up in a Depression that had disastrous effects not only in the USA but world-wide.

The Wall Street Crash was created by a loss of confidence as great as the over-confidence that fuelled the earlier boom. As share prices fell, people panicked and sold shares cheaply, causing prices to fall further. Banks ran out of money. Many people lost their savings. Many could not repay mortgages, loans or hire-purchase repayments. The boom had encouraged people to go into debt. Now they had no money for their repayments so they lost their homes and their possessions. They couldn't afford to buy goods, so many businesses failed, leaving more and more workers unemployed. Some of the homeless and unemployed set up shanty towns in many cities, which people called 'Hoovervilles', because they felt President Hoover's inaction had contributed to the situation. People urged the government to abandon *laissez faire* and act to help the economy and those without homes or work.

In this Key Topic you will study:

◉ the consequences of the Wall Street Crash 1929–30
◉ Hoover's reaction to the Great Depression
◉ the impact of the Depression on people's lives.

Bust!

Learning objectives

In this chapter you will learn about:
- the events of the Wall Street Crash
- the effects of the Wall Street Crash.

In September 1929, some investors, worried about the problems of the US economy, decided that the value of shares had gone as high as it could. They sold shares. The price of shares dropped. At first people were confident that they would go up again. They had in the past, as people bought lower priced shares at a bargain rate.

Collapse of confidence

This time, people did not buy. Prices continued to fall. More people sold shares. Prices continued to drop. By mid-October, panic set in. On 24 October, Black Thursday as it became known, there was panic selling all day, with people selling at huge losses. As news spread around the country, more and more people told their brokers to sell their shares as soon as possible. Until then, the stock exchange might handle 4–5 million shares on a busy day. On Black Thursday nearly 13m shares changed hands, and many more were offered for sale but not bought.

As soon as it became clear what was happening, a group of bankers agreed on a plan to calm things down: maybe they could stop the panic by investing money. They bought $250m worth of shares. This did slow panic selling on Friday, but everyone was expecting the next week to start badly, and it did.

On Monday 28 October, about 9m shares were traded. People and banks lost thousands of millions of dollars. The next day was even worse than Black Thursday. The bankers who had bought shares on Black Thursday to try to stabilise the situation were trying to sell these. Prices were dropping so fast that the ticker-tape telegraph system that connected brokers all around the USA to Wall Street could not keep up with the drop.

It became clear, years too late, that the crash was caused not so much by the big traders and bankers – who rushed in to try to stop the explosion with $250 million – but by the hundreds of thousands of small-timers who had invested mostly borrowed money. The huge Mount Everest of the 1929 stock market was a mountain of credit on a molehill of actual money.

Source A: *From* America, *written by Alastair Cooke in 1976.*

Source B: People flocking to the New York Stock Exchange, October, 1929. As soon as the panic set in, people rushed to sell their shares, at any price at all, pulling prices down still further.

Trying to keep control

On the afternoon of Tuesday 29 October, the committee that ran the stock market met to decide what to do. The stock market had crashed, despite the efforts of the bankers to stop it. It was a disaster. They had to do the best they could to avoid making things worse. Some wanted to stop trading at once, if people were not selling shares then prices could not fall any more. Others feared that closing the stock market down so suddenly would cause widespread riots. There had already been some riots in the rush to sell; it was important to keep things as calm as possible. It was also important to act quickly.

The committee decided not to shut the stock market down. They announced that it would keep trading until Thursday, then close until Monday. By the end of Tuesday, panic selling had stopped. Wednesday and Thursday saw more normal trading, and no riots. When the stock market re-opened on Monday, trading was back to normal. People hoped that prices would start to rise again. They didn't. It was not until 13 November that share prices hit their lowest and the next day began to creep up. By then, the damage was done. The panic had caused the Crash, and the Crash had appalling consequences for many banks, businesses and ordinary US citizens.

Banks

Banks that had been trading shares lost huge amounts of money. During, and just after, the Crash many people went to their bank to withdraw their savings. Those who went early enough were lucky. Many banks just didn't have enough money to pay out everyone's savings all at once. They went bankrupt and closed down. Many people never got the money they had saved so carefully. By 1933 just over 5,000 banks had closed. At just one of these banks, the Bank of New York, over 400,000 people lost their savings. Most of the people who had worked in these banks lost their jobs. The banks that survived needed money. People, and countries, that had borrowed money from them were asked to repay their loans, in full, at once. Many of them could not do this.

Businesses

When banks demanded the repayment of their loans, it was the last straw for many businesses. They went bankrupt because they could not repay their loans. Those that survived faced more problems.

- Banks were refusing to give businesses credit, money to cover the period between buying raw materials and selling the goods they made with them. Without credit, some factories could not function, so closed down.
- People stopped buying goods, because they could not afford them. Factories cut down on production, so made less money and needed fewer workers, so unemployment rose.

Company	3 March 1928	3 Sept 1929	13 Nov 1929
Woolworths	$1.81	$2.51	$0.52
Radio Corp.	$0.94	$5.05	$0.28
AT & T (telephone company)	$0.77	$3.04	$1.97
Westinghouse (electrical goods)	$0.92	$2.89	$1.02
General Motors (cars)	$1.40	$1.82	$0.36

Source C: *Share prices in 1928–9, from the* Wall Street Journal *newspaper.*

Did you know?

Immediately after the Wall Street Crash the papers were full of stories about 'jumpers', people who had lost millions in the Crash and committed suicide. There were a few famous cases, so people believed the suicide rate had risen sharply. In fact, there were far fewer than rumoured. Typically, a crowd gathered in New York following a rumour that a stockbroker was on the roof a nearby building about to jump. It turned out he was a builder, making repairs.

US citizens

Everyone in the USA was affected by the Crash, whether they had bought shares or not. This is because of the way the Crash hit banks and businesses. However, many people who had invested in shares on borrowed money, whether in a big way or not, were worst hit. Many went bankrupt. Those who had not bought shares were still hit by the Crash in several ways.

- They lost their savings if their banks went bankrupt.
- They lost their jobs if they worked for a business that closed.
- They lost their homes and farms if they could not pay their mortgage or their rent; either because they had lost their savings or because they had lost their job, or both.
- They lost their possessions if they couldn't pay the hire-purchase payments. Even if people had paid for their possessions in full, banks often took all saleable possessions to cover the loans or mortgages that customers could not repay.

Activities

1 a Make a timeline of the events outlined on pages 43 and 44

  b Show the information in Source C as a graph.

2 a If you had bought 100 shares in Radio Corp. on 3 March 1928, how much would they have cost?

  b What would they have been worth on 3 September 1929? How much profit would you have made?

  c How much would they have been worth on 13 November 1929? How much would you have lost?

3 Write a paragraph for a modern magazine article called 'Suicide and the Wall Street Crash of 1929'. Use Sources D and E as the basis for your article.

Source D: *From* The Great Crash 1929, *written by J K Galbraith in 1955.*

Year	Number of suicides per 100,000, USA
1925	12.1
1926	12.8
1927	13.3
1928	13.6
1929	14.0
1930	15.7
1931	16.8
1932	17.4
1933	15.9
1934	14.9

Source E: *A cartoon from a weekly magazine in November 1929 about the effects of the Wall Street Crash.*

Depression

The underlying economic problems of the USA and the fact that the boom had been based on such unrealistic expectations, meant the 'bust spiral' was especially rapid and unusually widespread. Businesses and farmers had kept overproducing and now faced a decline in demand at home and abroad and falling prices.

Because banks were in trouble, they could not help the economy to recover with loans. This made things worse. Such an **economic downturn** is called a 'depression'. The 1930s became known as the time of the Great Depression because of the scale of its effects. The people who were cushioned against it to some extent were:

- the very rich, who lost money but had still more
- gangsters, still making money out of Prohibition
- people who had savings in a bank that did not collapse
- people who did not lose their jobs or homes.

World-wide consequences

The Great Depression had word-wide effects. It set off a bust spiral, especially in Europe. The USA had lent its First World War allies money during and after the war – just under $10,000 million. These loans were being repaid, but even if they were asked to, no country could repay everything all at once. The US bought fewer goods from abroad. Other countries spent less on goods, to try to meet repayments. So they produced less, made less money, created unemployment – in short they too got pulled into depression. Between 1929 and 1934 world trade dropped by 66%. The fact that it set off a world-wide depression worsened the US depression.

Government reaction

The Republican government had made the economic situation worse. It had not caused the Great Depression, but it might have lessened the effects if it had acted sooner. Its *laissez faire* policies in the 1920s had let the stock market and businesses run themselves. It had not tried to control the high levels of credit. A few months before the Crash a new Republican President, Herbert Hoover, was elected. How would he deal with the crisis?

Year	Number unemployed	% of the total workforce
1927	1,890,000	4.1%
1928	2,080,000	4.4%
1929	1,550,000	3.2%
1930	4,340,000	8.7%
1931	8,020,000	15.9%
1932	12,060,000	23.6%
1933	12,830,000	24.9%

Source F: *Unemployment in the USA, from government statistics.*

Year	Cotton price in dollars per lb	Wheat price dollars a bushel
1927	20.19	1.19
1928	17.89	1.00
1929	16.78	1.04
1930	9.46	0.67
1931	5.66	0.39
1932	6.52	0.38
1933	10.20	0.74

Source G: *Cotton and wheat prices in the USA, from government statistics.*

examzone
Top tip!

In questions about *causes* or *effects* (like questions 2 and 3) the top marks usually go to an answer which shows the links between the factors. It might help to make a mind map of the links as part of your planning, to keep the links straight in your mind while you write your answer.

Activities

1 Events like the Wall Street Crash can be represented as 'spiral diagrams' like the one below.

   Copy the diagram, filling in the labels (make sure you give yourself enough space to write the full label).

   - *People sell shares*
   - *More people want to sell than to buy*
   - *People worried share prices will fall more*

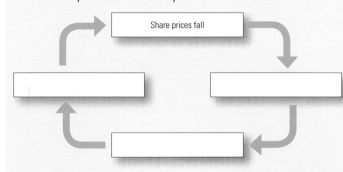

Share prices fall

2 Make a list of the various ways the Wall Street Crash might affect a cotton farmer in the South with a mortgage on his farm, $100 of savings in the bank and $200 invested in shares.

3 Draw a second spiral diagram, this time using the following four steps (you will need to sort them into the right order).

   - *Fewer manufactured goods made*
   - *Fewer manufactured goods bought*
   - *Fewer people have money to spend*
   - *Fewer workers employed in manufacturing*

4 Draw similar spiral diagrams to show:

   a the effect of a rise in unemployment (see Source F)

   b the reactions of a farmer to a fall in prices (see Source G).

Source H: *A Chicago 'soup kitchen', 16 November 1930. This one was set up by Al Capone (see page 32) who gave $300 a day to feed about 3,500 unemployed people three meals a day.*

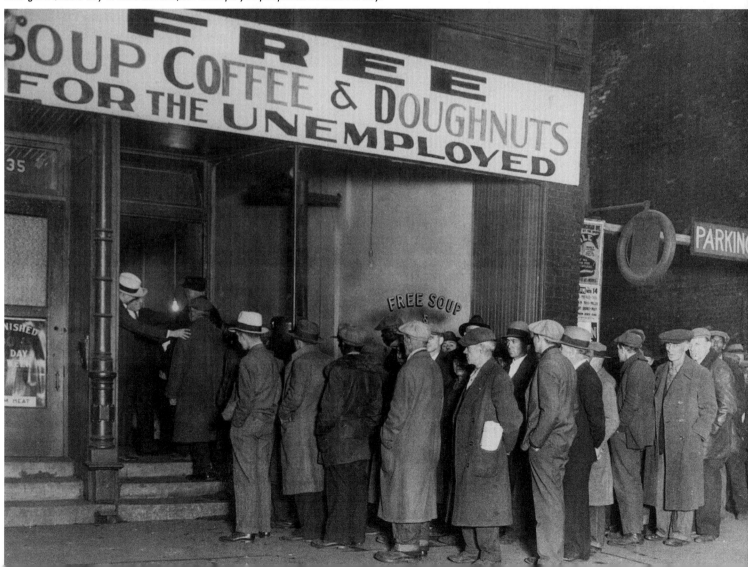

Hoover's reaction

> **Learning objectives**
>
> In this chapter you will learn about:
> - how the government reacted to economic problems 1929–31
> - the influence of Hoover.

Hoover was a Republican, so seemed unlikely to suggest a change in government policy. He believed in *laissez faire*. He also believed that government help made people weak and dependent. In one of his pre-election speeches he had praised the 'rugged individualism' of the American people – how they managed their own lives without relying on others, such as the government, for help. However, even Republicans had to face the fact that the economy was not putting itself right when left to itself.

Helping the economy

After Hoover became President in 1929, even before the Crash in October, he set up the Federal Farm Board. Hoover knew that many farmers had been in financial difficulty ever since the end of the war and tariffs (see page 10) had made their situation worse. He saw that they needed government help, despite his hopes that the situation would put itself right. The Federal Farm Board bought up surplus grain and cotton from farmers all over the country and stored it for later re-sale.

Hoover's government cut taxes in 1929, so people would have more money to spend. It put more money into government building projects, which created more jobs. Hoover also set up a temporary group called the President's Emergency Committee for Employment (PECE), which encouraged local initiatives. It organised campaigns to collect money for the unemployed and persuade businesses not to cut their workforce. In 1931, PECE became a permanent organisation, re-named the President's Organisation for Unemployment Relief (POUR). The government was beginning to see that the economic situation was not improving and that it would need to step in. So, in 1932 it did set up some organisations, some of which had money to help those in need. However, 1932 was a presidential election year, and Hoover may have been motivated by the need to get votes.

Source A: *A pro-Hoover badge from the 1928 election campaign. In 1919, Hoover had made a name for himself running the American Relief Administration which organised food and other vital supplies for war-torn Europe, even Germany and communist Russia.*

During the past three weeks I have been working with members of the administration, to study the problems of unemployment and relief likely to confront us over the coming winter and the organisation needed to meet the situation. While many improvements seem promising, the problem, whatever it may be, will be met. Local, State and Federal authorities, and the large number of relief and charitable organisations, cooperated to handle the problem successfully last winter.

Source B: *From a press statement by Hoover, 7 August 1931. The President's Organisation for Unemployment Relief was set up on 19 August.*

Steps taken

July 1929 Federal Farm Board: $500m to buy up surplus agricultural products. By 1932, the money was spent and the Board was disbanded. To start with, the food they bought was destroyed rather than used to feed the unemployed.

June 1930 Smoot-Hawley tariff: increased tariffs on imported goods to try to make people buy things made in the USA, and so keep more US workers in jobs. It caused a drop in both imports and exports, further damaging trade, and made things worse, not better.

1931 National Credit Corporation (NCC): a private organisation funded by healthy banks and businesses to lend money to less secure ones to save them from bankruptcy and restore confidence. The NCC started with $500m and had lent just $10m by the end of the year. Because it wasn't doing enough, the government replaced it with the RFC.

January 1932 Reconstruction Finance Corporation (RFC): the replacement for NCC under government control, also lent money to railroads and businesses.

July 1932 Emergency Relief and Construction Act: extended RFC lending to farming and public works. It had an extra $300m to give to states for relief.

July 1932 Federal Home Loan Bank Act: supervised banks and other lenders. Had a fund to lend money to people who had problems paying loans. It had 41,000 applicants for help. Only three were accepted.

The papers get us all excited over one or a dozen different problems in this country. There's only one problem – at least 7,000,000 people are out of work. Our only problem is to see that every man that wants to is able to work.

So here we are, in a country with more wheat and corn and money in the bank; more cotton, more everything, and yet we've got people starving. We'll be the only nation in the history of the world that ever went to the poor house in an automobile.

Source C: *From a radio broadcast by the US comic Will Rodgers on 18 October 1931. POUR organised this appeal for donations to the relief funds set up in each of the states.*

Activities

1 Draw up a table like the one below. From the tax cut of 1930 to the 1932 Federal Home Loan Bank, enter each policy of Hoover's government, and fill in the rest of the row.

2 Think about the question in the Build better answers Box.

   a Which policies would you use to answer this question? Pick at least four.

   b What details would you add to explain how your chosen policies show the government's response to the problems?

Policy	Date	How it was expected to help	The effect it had
Tax cut	1930	Give people more money to spend	Did not work. The money went

examzone

Build better answers

Exam question: Describe how the government responded to the problems of the USA between 1929 and 1932. **(6 marks)**

You need to describe the key features of government policy between those dates. There are two levels. The more features you give in a level, the more marks you will get.

▪ **Basic answers (level 1)** will give a list of features without details (for example, *... at first they did not want to provide government help*).

▲ **Better answers (level 2)** will give a list of features with details to support them. (For example, *... did not want to provide government help, they thought this would weaken people, so Hoover set up PECE to persuade Americans to give to charities to help the unemployed. They did more when they realised private help was failing, so the NCC was replaced by the RFC because the NCC only loaned $10m to banks.*)

Living through the Depression

> ### Learning objectives
>
> In this chapter you will learn about:
> - the effects of the Depression, especially in the cities
> - the development of the Dust Bowl.

The people hit hardest by the Depression were the poor, the homeless and the unemployed (many people were all of these things). By the time the government decided to do something to help them, it was harder for them to get help as there were so many people who needed it.

The unemployed

Until 1932, there was very little government help for the unemployed. Some rich people (including Al Capone, the gangster) set up soup kitchens to feed people in the towns they lived in (see page 47), but this help was very patchy. Otherwise, people had to rely on relief provided by charities that collected money and set up small soup kitchens or shelters. Some charities gave a small amount of money each week to 'needy' families of the unemployed. The government relief agencies set up in 1932 were swamped by requests for help, so they made very harsh rules. Social workers checked if people were really unemployed, but they also went into their homes to see if they had anything they could sell to get money for food before they gave them any money. Sometimes, they even weighed the children in the family to see if they were starving enough to be fed at government soup kitchens.

The homeless

Many homeless people went to towns and cities hoping to find work and somewhere to live. Most did not succeed, for the cities were experiencing unemployment and homelessness too. People began to call the '**shanty towns**' that sprung up on the edges of towns and cities, 'Hoovervilles', after the President who they felt was letting them down by repeatedly assuring them that the Depression was a temporary problem.

The father was a railroad man who had lost his job. My supervisor had told me I really had to see the poverty. If the family needed clothing, I was to investigate how much clothing they had. So I looked into this man's closet. He was so insulted. He said, 'Why are you doing this?' I remember his feeling of humiliation … this terrible humiliation. He said, 'I really haven't anything to hide, but if you really must look into it …' I could see he was very proud. He was deeply humiliated. And I was too.

Source A: *Eileen Barth, a relief worker, interviewed about one of her first cases, in 1931. From* Hard Times, *written by Studs Terkel in 1970.*

In 1932 officials in Birmingham, Alabama, sounded a warning in their application for federal aid: 'Unless relief is immediately given, the relief agencies in the city of Birmingham and in Jefferson County [the area around Birmingham] will be forced to stop their relief work and no alternative can be expected other than widespread starvation or disorder.'

Source B: *From* The American Dole, *written by Jeff Singleton in 2000.*

There is not a garbage-dump in Chicago that is not haunted by the hungry. Last summer, in the hot weather when the smell was sickening and the flies were thick, there were a hundred people a day coming to one of the dumps. A widow who used to do housework and laundry, but now had no work at all, fed herself and her fourteen-year-old son on garbage. Before she picked up the meat, she would always take off her glasses so that she couldn't see the maggots.

Source C: *Written by Edmund Wilson in the magazine* New Republic, *published in February 1933.*

Activities

1 a What was a Hooverville?

b Describe what you can see in Source D.

c Do you think the people who lived there were supporters of President Hoover? Give reasons for your answer.

2 Turn Source B into a six-word text message from a Birmingham official to the federal government.

3 You are a radio reporter visiting the USA in late 1931. Write the text for a 90-second radio broadcast, telling people back in Britain what is happening in the Depression in the USA. Use the text and sources from pages 46–49 to make a list of the key features before writing the text. Think about what details or personal stories you can include to make your report more vivid.

examzone

Watch out!

When discussing the effects of an event, be careful not to give the impression that events affected all people in the same way. Don't say 'The Depression made people unemployed', say 'The Depression caused high levels of unemployment. Many people lost their jobs.'

Source D: *A 'Hooverville' in Seattle, Washington State, 1933.*

During and immediately after the war, the USA became a major producer of wheat and other cereal crops. They carried on producing at a high rate even when demand fell, so causing a drop in prices that caused a lot of hardship (see pages 10, 18 and 46). Some of the land that was converted from grazing to growing wheat was not really suitable. It had been made to work, but problems were building up. The Great Plains in the middle of the USA was the most extreme example. Years of ploughing and planting, with no rest for the soil or adding nutrients had damaged it. During the 1920s it rained more than usual over the Great Plains and this helped to minimise the damage done. However, farmers were suffering, not only because of the drop in demand and prices, but also because crops were growing less well in the soil.

Creating a dust bowl

In 1931, drought hit. The rain slowed, then stopped. The soil dried out and many farmers lost most of their crop. They had little or nothing to sell in order to live through the winter and buy seed for the next year. The drought continued. Then the windstorms came. The wind whipped up the dusty soil and carried it hundreds of miles, as a huge dark cloud. Farmers lost the soil they needed to grow crops. The dust storms, called 'black blizzards' could reduce visibility to just a few metres. There were 14 in 1932 and 38 in 1933.

Migrant workers

In many farming families the men and teenage boys took to the road, hoping to find work somewhere else to support their families. They joined an existing group of people, often called 'hobos', who moved around the country looking for work. They moved either on foot or by riding illegally on trains, often in goods trucks. The number of hobos rose during the Depression. It is hard to estimate their numbers, but most historians agree there were 1–2 million hobos in the early 1930s. Some migrant workers found work, others stayed in one city and kept looking. They often had to eat in soup kitchens and live in Hoovervilles or 'flophouses' – cheap rooms (usually shared) in slum housing.

An entire generation of adolescents spent time on the road and away from family and home. Some followed the harvest seasons of various fruits and grains across the country and became temporary labour for farmers. Others got meals and a free night's lodging from mission churches. Most spent time in hobo camps, living on stolen or begged food.

Source E: *From the Ulys Family Oral History Collection, a collection of hobo reminiscences from the 1930s.*

18 November 1928 The bank failed last Friday, so the whole community is pretty down. Since the 1 July hailstorms, the farmers around here have already taken out about $50,000 (some of it borrowed) and have nothing to put in. Now the bank savings they counted on for living expenses over the winter and seed for the spring is gone. Our student association lost the $124 we raised for new basketball uniforms. The teachers lost all the money they had saved.

Source F: *From* Dust Bowl Diary, *Ann Marie Low's memories of growing up in the Dust Bowl, written in 1984.*

During the thirties, serious drought threatened a great part of the USA. From 1931, it centred on the Great Plains. In that year Montana and the Dakotas became almost as dry as a desert. Farmers there (and almost everywhere) watched the scorched earth crack open, heard the gray grass crunch underfoot and worried about how they would be able to pay their bills.

Source G: *From* Dust Bowl, *written by Donald Worster in 2004.*

Activities

1 Write a sentence to explain how Source F suggests that the Depression was not just about the Wall Street Crash.

2 In this question you have to *find the link*. It is designed to help you think about *consequences*. For example: **First World War   Dust Bowl**

In the First World War there was a shortage of food, so US farmers ploughed up a lot of grazing land in the mid-west to grow wheat. This land was affected by drought, and because there was no grass to keep the soil together, much of it blew away in dust storms. They called the area the Dust Bowl.

Now explain the link between:

a Depression   Migrant workers

b President Hoover   Hoovervilles

c Depression   Increase in family breakdown and divorce

d Bank failure   Hobos

exam zone
Top tip!

In your answer to the 16-mark question – like the one on the right – you will be marked on the quality of your writing and on your spelling, punctuation and grammar. Take time to check your writing and ensure it is accurate in spelling, punctuation and grammar. For a question like this, make sure you can spell words such as: mortgage, economy/economic, bankrupt, business, Depression, hire purchase, *laissez faire*, individualism, financial, federal, corporate and Hoovervilles.

exam zone
Build better answers

Exam question: Was unemployment the most significant consequence of the Depression? Explain your answer.

You may use the following in your answer:
• rising unemployment
• rising homelessness.
You must also include information of your own.   (16 marks)
This question is about *consequences*.

■ **A basic answer (level 1)** makes a simple generalisation about causes.

● **A good answer (level 2)** agrees and/or disagrees with the proposition in the question but does not explain the impact of other suggested consequences (for example … *unemployment was a big problem because the unemployed and their families needed help from charities, or later the government. But homelessness was a huge problem too.*). A more complete answer will examine more than two causes.

▲ **A better answer (level 3)** will explain the causes discussed.

▲ **An excellent answer (level 4)** will prioritise the causes, or see links between them (for example, … *There were many consequences, which all linked together and unemployment was a significant one, because it could set off other consequences. So the unemployed could often not keep up mortgage payments, or hire-purchase payments, so they had their homes and possessions taken away and became unemployed AND homeless….*).

Make sure you write accurately – there are 4 extra marks available for spelling, grammar and punctuation in these questions

Source H: *A 'black blizzard' building up on the Great Plains in the 1930s.*

Government unpopularity

> ### Learning objectives
> In this chapter you will learn about:
> - reaction to Hoover's policies
> - the election of 1932.

By 1932, presidential election year, Hoover was very unpopular. He had not produced the 'chicken in every pot' of his election slogan. He said things were getting better and everyone was coping – when it wasn't and they weren't. They felt he clung to *laissez faire*, when it clearly wasn't working.

Rising resentment

Hoover was beginning to realise that *laissez faire* wasn't working, and he started to move towards government intervention. But these first steps just caused resentment. The poor resented the tax cuts which Hoover intended as a way to keep people spending, but which they saw as favouring the rich. They also resented the RFC (see page 49) because they felt it was helping the rich – Hoover intended it to restore stability in banks and businesses. They felt the government federal work projects came too late (unemployment had reached over 12 million) and provided too few jobs.

Meanwhile, businesses resented the tariff increase. US exports dropped from $2,341 million dollars in 1929 to $784 million dollars in 1932. This did not help businesses or farmers at all. Relief groups, state and privately funded, resented the fact that federal government acted as if they were coping with the needs of the unemployed and the poor, while in fact they were losing the battle to keep people from starvation. All this resentment meant Hoover got little credit for his moves towards federal intervention.

There were more and more protests in towns and cities across the USA. By 1932, these often ended in violence between protesters and the police. Generally, by 1932, the police were far less tolerant of the unemployed and people living in Hoovervilles. They began to see them as criminals. Certainly desperation drove some to steal.

Source A: *A cartoon quotes from a statement made by Hoover in July 1932. A cyclone cellar was somewhere to hide from tornados – the cartoonist is implying that Hoover was hiding from the Depression.*

 Hoover: what's your verdict?

Making judgements is one of the things historians do. Obviously, these judgements have to be based on evidence, so what evidence should we use to make a judgement about whether Hoover was a success?

Look back over pages 42–53 and make two lists: *Things that show Hoover was a success* and *Things that show Hoover was a failure*.

The Bonus Army

In 1924, the US government gave those who had fought in the First World War a bonus calculated on how long they had been in the army. They paid those who were owed $50 at once. The money to pay everyone else went into a fund to pay out in 1945. Many people who were due a bonus in 1945 were hit by the Depression in some way. Many were unemployed and living in Hoovervilles (see pages 50–51).

In May 1932, about 15,000 of them marched to Washington, some with their families, to ask to be paid their bonuses at once, because they needed them. This 'Bonus Army', sometime known as 'the Bonus Marchers', set up a Hooverville just across the river from Capitol Hill, where the federal government buildings were. More marchers arrived, setting up camps in deserted buildings and on waste land. Hoover's official called the Bonus Army 'a rabble', but the camps were well run. The government's concern was more because the men in these camps were ex-soldiers and could fight.

Hoover's reaction

Hoover said the government could not pay the bonuses in 1932. The House of Representatives voted to do so anyway, but they were overruled by the Senate which, on 17 July, voted not to pay by 62 votes to 18. Hoover offered the Bonus Army loans to go home. About 5,000 of the marchers accepted. The rest stayed and continued to demonstrate; they got a lot of sympathy. The government was afraid of violence. On 28 July, they told the police to clear the Bonus Army out of their Hoovervilles. The Bonus Army refused to go. Hoover sent in the army to clear them out. Fighting broke out. Four Bonus marchers were killed and over 1,000 were injured.

The sources will often be useful.

In pairs, test each of the two statements below against the evidence you have collected. Is either of them right? Can both of them be right?

a Hoover did as much as he could to solve the crisis, he intervened more than any president before him had done.

b Hoover was a failure, and people at the time knew he was a failure. All you need to know is that he lost the election 42 states to 6.

Hoover had not talked to the press about the Bonus Army before he called in the troops. Afterwards however, he called a press conference to justify his actions. He said that over 5,000 of the Bonus marchers had taken advantage of the loans to go home. He insisted that many of those who remained had been investigated and found to be communists or criminals, not war veterans. Not everyone was convinced by this.

Activity

1 a In pairs, list five reasons why Hoover was unpopular by the time he ran for re-election.

  b Now decide which is the most important of these reasons. Turn it into a slogan Roosevelt could use for his election campaign.

Source B: *A drawing published in a newspaper shortly after 28 July 1932.*

HERE·LIES
WILLIAM·HUSHKA
WORLD·WAR·VETERAN
KILLED
IN·THE·BATTLE
AGAINST·STARVATION
AT·WASHINGTON·D.C.
JULY · 28TH · 1932
BY·ORDER·OF
HERBERT·HOOVER

We Shall Not Forget

Know Zone
Unit 2C - Key Topic 3

In the Unit 2 exam, you will have to answer six questions: Question 1(a), (b), (c) and (d); either Question 2(a) or Question 2(b); and either Question 3(a) or Question 3(b).

You only have an hour and 15 minutes to answer these questions. Use the number of marks available for each question to help you judge how long to spend on each answer. Here we are going to look at questions 2(a) and (b). Allow about 12 minutes for this question.

examzone

Build better answers

Question 2 (a)

Tip: Question 2 will ask you to use your knowledge to explain how something changed or developed. In the examination you can choose to answer whichever of Question 2(a) or (b) you like the most. Do not do both (a) and (b) as you will only be awarded marks for one of them.

a Explain how the Wall Street Crash developed into the Depression in the USA, 1929–32. (8 marks)

Student answer	Comments
In the 1929 Wall Street Crash the value of shares fell and everyone lost their money because of this firms had to sack workers and there were millions of people unemployed.	Oh dear. This isn't very good. It is true that the value of shares fell, and that many people lost their jobs, but the candidate hasn't explained the link between them. The candidate hasn't explained about the problems with loans and credit, and how this affected businesses. It isn't really true to say everybody lost their money either. This would be a Level 1 answer.

Let's rewrite the answer with the detail added.

In the 1929 Wall Street Crash the value of shares fell. Many people had borrowed money to buy shares, and their shares were now worth much less than the money they borrowed. Lots of these people could not pay back their loans, and they were bankrupt. Some banks started to fail, and people had less money to spend. Because of this fewer things were bought, so fewer were made, and so businesses needed fewer worker, So this is how firms had to sack workers, and why there were millions of people unemployed.	There is more that could be said here, but the candidate has now explained how the problems on the stock market led to problems with banks, and to there being less spending, and how this moves into the bust spiral. This is a level 3 answer.

Question 2 (b)

Let us now look at Question 2 (b). This time, instead of looking at a student answer and comment, we will trace the thought processes of the student as they write their answer.

A suitable question would be:

b Explain how President Hoover dealt with the distress and poverty caused by the Depression, 1929–32.   (8 marks)

Student's thought processes	Student's answer
Why the dates 1929–1932? That's from the Wall Street Crash until Hoover lost the presidential election. What about 'distress and poverty'? I know what Hoover did, but I'd probably better just state the problem. I don't suppose the marks are for that, though, so I'll keep it short.	After the Wall Street Crash in October 1929, the American economy went into a bust spiral. People who lost their jobs or their savings could not keep up their rent or mortgage payments, and millions lost their homes. Shanty towns called Hoovervilles grew up in the main cities.
Now I need to talk about Hoover's ideas about what to do, and then some of his policies.	Hoover believed in the free market and *laissez faire*. He thought that if the Federal Government started to help people it would weaken the country in the long term. He also believed that the Depression would end quickly. In 1930 he reduced taxes, hoping that people would spend more money, and so save jobs or create new ones. He also set up his emergency committee, PECE, but all this did was encourage the states and the rich to help the unemployed. In 1931 he raised tariffs to make imports more expensive, so that people would buy US-made goods. This didn't work, because other countries set up tariffs and the US lost more exports.
So now I think I have explained at least two ways. That should get me top level. Is there anything else I can add? Yes – the policies before the election. Then I'll add a short summary.	In 1932 things were getting worse, and Hoover was up for re-election. He did a bit more. First he set up the RFC to loan money to banks and businesses to stop them going out of business. Then he set up the Federal Homes Loan Bank to lend people money to stop them losing their houses, but it only made three loans. Hoover didn't do much, because he thought the best way to solve the problem was to let people solve it themselves. He became very unpopular.

Key Topic 4: Roosevelt and the New Deal 1933–41

As soon as Roosevelt became president, in March 1933, he set in motion the New Deal that he had promised the American people. He began by telling Congress that he felt the situation was as dangerous as any war, so he asked to meet with them in special session (so called because it was during part of the year when Congress did not normally meet) and suggest laws to solve the crisis. During the first 100 days of his presidency, Congress passed every law Roosevelt suggested. These laws ploughed billions of federal dollars into providing work, relief for the poor and unemployed, stability for the financial system and help for farmers. Roosevelt believed it was the government's job to make the economy work and help the unemployed.

Roosevelt set up agencies to run various aspects of federal relief. They were often called the 'Alphabet Agencies' because they were usually referred to by the first letter of each word in their name (for example, 'the Works Progress Administration' became 'the WPA'). But Roosevelt and the New Deal faced opposition from various groups including businessmen, Republicans and the Supreme Court.

Did the New Deal work? It had failures and successes, but it changed the atmosphere in 1934, and helped millions out of poverty. By 1941, it was clear that the country was recovering. By this time, however, the New Deal had been helped by a need for much greater production because the world was at war again and the USA was once more producing arms and supplies for itself and its European allies.

In this Key Topic you will study:

- the nature of the New Deal
- opposition to the New Deal
- the extent of recovery.

Roosevelt

Electing a president

In the 1932 presidential elections, Franklin D Roosevelt (often called FDR) stood as the Democratic candidate against Hoover. He promised:

'I pledge you, I pledge myself, to a new deal for the American people.'

He was welcomed almost everywhere he went on his campaign. Hoover's government had offered too little help, too late. His handling of the Bonus Army had made him even more unpopular. In his presidential campaign he was often booed and even had rotten fruit thrown at him. FDR won 42 of the 48 states.

Roosevelt as president

In Roosevelt's first speech as president, on 4 March 1933, he laid out his aims for the first few months, assuring people, 'we have nothing to fear but fear itself.' By this he meant it was important to rebuild confidence. He said the most important tasks were:

● to get people working
● to rebuild confidence in banks and shares
● to provide relief for those in need.

Roosevelt abandoned *laissez faire*. He said the government would spend federal money on projects right across the USA. He said the government would also put controls on banks and businesses. During his first hundred days in office he pushed through emergency laws to do this, indeed his first act as president was to close all banks for seven days.

Roosevelt felt that confidence would be rebuilt more quickly if people understood what the government was doing and why it was doing it. On 12 March 1933 he began a series of radio broadcasts that became known as 'fireside chats' because of the way he spoke as if he was a friend, dropping in to explain something.

Roosevelt's New Deal was built around three pillars, Relief, Recovery and Reform. Relief provided short-term and temporary support to those out of work or in financial difficulty. The medium-term goal was Recovery. This would put the country back onto an economic even-footing.

This would then allow Reform to take hold with the long-term aim of ensuring that this kind of deep Depression would not happen again.

Fireside chats

FDR's first fireside chat was about why he had closed the banks. Unlike Hoover, he was careful to point out the difficulties ahead. He told people he was going to reform the banks and relied on their 'intelligent support'. He asked them to trust the banks when they reopened and not take out money in a panic. They didn't panic. They trusted him, if not the banks. These chats would feature all through his presidency.

> Our first task is to put people to work. It can be accomplished in part by the government itself recruiting – treating the task as we would treat a war emergency... The task can be helped by definite efforts to raise the values of agricultural products, and with this the power to purchase the output of our cities... It can be helped by preventing the tragedy of the growing loss through foreclosure of our small homes and farms... It can be helped by unifying relief activities, which today are often scattered, uneconomical, unequal. We must act quickly.

Source A: *From President Roosevelt's inaugural speech, 4 March 1933.*

Activities

1 Make a list of all the things suggested in Source A that were a change from the policies of Hoover's government.

2 a In pairs, decide what the biggest change of direction in government policy was, as outlined by Roosevelt at the start of his presidency.

 b Design a slogan of not more than eight words that sums this up.

The Hundred Days

Learning objectives

In this chapter you will learn about:
- the legislation of the Hundred Days
- what the Alphabet Agencies did.

Between 9 March and 16 June 1933 (the 100 days), Roosevelt and Congress passed laws focused on recovery; stopping the sharp decline of the Depression with emergency legislation. They began with the Emergency Banking Act. This agreed to the bank closure Roosevelt had ordered on 5 March and set up investigations into their finances so that only the financially sound banks could re-open.

The table opposite shows the major legislation of the Hundred Days and the so-called Alphabet Agencies it created. Many agencies were set up to run for only a year or two. Extra taxation was agreed to help raise money.

There was no deliberate attempt to change the US political system by enlarging federal authority over the states. The guiding idea was federal-state co-operation, with the federal government providing funds to states, usually matching the amount the state provided.

Source A: *From an article on Roosevelt and the New Deal written by D K Adams in 1979.*

Exam-style question

Explain how the Hundred Days legislation changed the situation of the unemployed. (8 marks)

Source B: *Dinner time at a CCC camp in Lancaster, California. The 200 men at the camp were building roads in the forest so that fire engines could get around more easily to put out forest fires.*

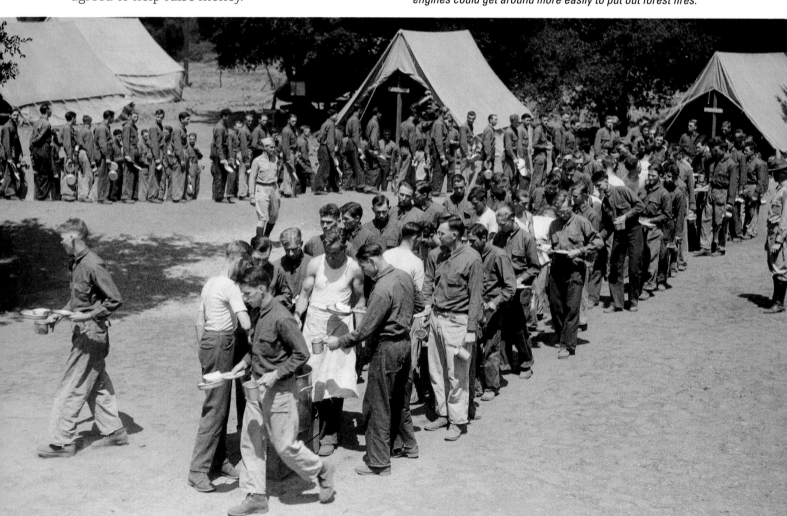

The legislation of the first 100 days	
Date and act	**What it did**
9 March 1933 Emergency Banking Act	Set up federal inspection of closed banks; 'financially sound' could reopen. By 12 March, about 5,000 banks had reopened; more followed. Some banks did not reopen, but the inspections restored confidence. There was no rush to take out money.
20 March 1933 Economy Act	Reorganised the administration to save 25% of running costs and cut wages for government workers by 15% – giving the government more money to spend on relief.
22 March 1933 Beer and Wine Revenue Act	Effectively ended Prohibition by changing the definition of 'intoxicating liquor' while waiting for the official end by the passing of the 21st Amendment to the Constitution. This allowed beer and wine to be made and sold – and taxed – so making more money to spend on relief. The 21st Amendment officially ended Prohibition on 5 December 1933.
31 March 1933 Reforestation Relief Act	Set up the Civilian Conservation Corps (CCC). Young men aged 17 to 23, volunteers, went to camps (several in every state) to work on replanting the forests and digging ditches and reservoirs. The camps were run by the army. The workers earned $30 a month: $2/_3$ of it was sent home.
12 May 1933 Federal Emergency Relief Administration Act (FERA)	This had a fund of $3 billion, to give to states for relief. FERA set up the Civil Works Administration (CWA) to organise public works (building schools, roads, bridges, dams etc.) to get the unemployed working.
12 May 1933 Agricultural Adjustment Act	Set up the Agricultural Adjustment Administration (AAA) to give subsidies (payments) to farmers to encourage them to grow less and so reduce overproduction. It regulated the major crops: corn, wheat, cotton, rice, peanuts, tobacco and milk. It began by buying up surplus crops and animals to push prices up.
18 May 1933 Tennessee Valley Authority Act	This set up the Tennessee Valley Authority (TVA), to run land development in the Tennessee Valley, which covered 104,000 sq km in seven states. It built dams to make electricity, and then ran power all over its states, especially to rural areas.
27 May 1933 Federal Security Act	Set down new rules for the stock market to make another crash less likely.
6 June 1933 National Employment Systems Act	Set up the US Employment Service, a government-run service to help the unemployed find work.
13 June 1933 Home Owners' Relief Act	Set up loans or helped to extend the mortgages (so reducing the payments each month) for people having trouble paying their mortgages.
16 June 1933 National Industrial Relief Act	Set up the National Recovery Administration (NRA) which set codes to regulate working conditions. It laid down a minimum wage, an 8-hour day and prohibited child labour. Joining the NRA was voluntary. Businesses that signed up to the scheme showed a blue eagle symbol in their window. Also set up the Public Works Administration (PWA) with $3.3 billion to fund public works.
16 June 1933 Farm Credit Act	Set up the Farm Credit Administration (FCA) which lent farmers money to help with loans on their home or equipment.
June 1933 Glass-Steagall Banking Act	Set up the Federal Deposit Insurance Corporation (FDIC), which gave government insurance to savings in government-approved banks and regulated their stock market activities.

Activities

1 **a** In pairs, write the name of each act of the Hundred Days and its date on a piece of card. Sort the cards into two categories: 'raising money' and 'spending money'. Write down the two categories, and how many cards are in each pile. Discuss why the result you got might show problems waiting to happen.

 b Now organise the cards into piles according to whether they are dealing with *unemployment*, *finance*, or *welfare*. Write down the categories and how many in each. If some fit into more than one category, count them in each one. **(Save these cards, you will need them again.)**

2 Write a short report for the *New York Times*, summing up the legislation of the Hundred Days, saying what it seems to be trying to achieve and how.

examzone

Top tip!

When asked to explain aims or key features, it will help if you start by making a simple bulleted list, so you don't miss any of the basic points. Then write the answer, being careful to add examples from your knowledge for each item. So, when asked to consider Roosevelt's aims in the Hundred Days, you can give examples for the laws passed in that time to support your list of aims. Give at least three examples.

Once FDR felt the banks and the stock market were under control, laws and agency money focussed on improving agriculture, industry, unemployment and welfare.

Agriculture

Prohibition was ended, helping farmers who grew crops that could be used to make alcohol. The Farm Credit Administration lent farmers money to help them buy equipment or meet their bills. The Agricultural Adjustment Agency (AAA) bought surplus produce, regulated faming production and gave farmers subsidies to encourage them to grow less, so stopping over-production.

Industry

The NRA wrote codes for wages and working conditions, including the right to belong to a union. There were over 700 codes, affecting about 22 million workers. No one had to follow these codes, but people were encouraged to favour businesses that were part of the scheme.

Unemployment

US Employment Service offices across the country helped people to find work. Federal agencies, such as the CWA, the PWA and the CCC (see page 61), provided work on federal projects for millions of unemployed. By January 1934, CWA projects employed about 4 million people.

Welfare

Some government agencies (such as the AAA) provided relief as part of their work. Others extended the basic government aid set up under Hoover. They helped with rent and food bills, or ran soup kitchens.

The Agencies at work

Each Alphabet Agency had a federal budget. States applied for money from this budget for projects. The agencies gave money to well-planned projects that gave the greatest amount of help as quickly as possible. An example of this is the Tennessee Valley Authority. It provided work for the unemployed, providing help for the area. Building dams on the river stopped flooding and provided a hydro-electric power industry. Workers ran electric lines all over the area. CCC workers slowed down soil erosion and set up fertiliser plants to supply local farmers. Families that had to move for the dams were resettled on new farms and taught good farming practices. However, the Agencies did not treat all alike. Many discriminated against African American workers and sharecroppers ,who were mainly black, often missed out on money from the likes of the AAA.

By the time TVA was set up in 1933, fertile topsoil had gone from over a million acres in the Valley. What was left was dry clay, useless even for growing most weeds. The Valley's main cash crops (cotton, corn, tobacco) had drained the soil of its nutrients. Worse, traditional agriculture, which often involved planting on hillsides and letting fields lie bare in winter, left topsoil open to the weather. The rain that watered crops also carried the soil away. Farm yields were lower every year.

Source C: *A description of the Tennessee Valley in 1933, from the TVA website in 2009.*

Did you know?

Roosevelt was convinced that federal and state spending would 'prime the pump' to the US economy and rebuild confidence. Water pumps drew water up from underground by pumping a handle. Sometimes they ran dry and had to be started by putting water in. This was called 'priming' the pump. You got far more water out than you put in. Roosevelt meant the government had to put money into the economy to start it flowing again.

examzone
Watch out!

Don't confuse the PWA (Public Works Administration) with the WPA (Works Progress Administration). The PWA was the first organisation, set up in 1933 with a fixed budget to spend on public works. The WPA was set up in 1935 and gave funding for many smaller projects, as well as public works. It also provided training in many kinds of jobs.

Activities

1   You need the cards you used for question 1 on page 61.

   a   Make a new card for each of the alphabet agencies.

   b   Sort all the cards into two groups: those which were about *relief* (helping people) and those that were about *reform* (changing things for the long term). Make a two-column table, headed *relief* and *reform* and list each of the cards under the appropriate heading.

   c   In pairs, compare your answers. Are they the same?

2   Now draw up a table with four headings: *agriculture, industry, unemployment* and *welfare*. In pairs, sort the cards into piles for these headings, and write down your answers in the table.

3   **a**   What can you learn from Source C about the problems of the Tennessee Valley?

   b   How did the TVA try to solve these problems?

4   **a**   What level is this answer to the question in the Build better answers box?

     The Alphabet Agencies helped people with the problems they had because of the Depression. They were set up as part of the New Deal. The Tennessee Valley Authority helped the farmers because it taught them to plant crops which would help to improve the soil.

   b   Copy the answer above **and add to it** so that it is an answer which gets full marks (remember, for full marks you need three points, each with supporting detail).

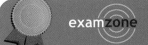

Build better answers

Exam question: Describe how the Alphabet Agencies worked. (6 marks)

Your exam paper will always have a question like this one, which tests your ability to select and communicate factual information.

■   **A basic answer (level 1)** will give points without detail. (For example, *The Alphabet Agencies ran projects to get people working.*)

●   **A good answer (level 2)** will give details to support each point. (For example, *The PWA got people working by giving grants to projects that created employment and the TVA was planned to supply work and electricity and advise farmers on farming methods that didn't cause erosion.*)

▲   **An excellent answer (full marks)** would give three points, each with supporting detail.

Source D: *Workers on a farm in California, photographed in September 1933.*

Opposition

Learning objectives

In this chapter you will learn about:
- reasons for opposition to the New Deal
- effects of this opposition.

The New Deal was popular with many people. President Roosevelt had millions of letters of support during his presidency. However, he also faced opposition from the very beginning. Why?

Wasting money?

No federal government had ever spent as much money as Roosevelt's. Many politicians worried the government would never be able to pay off the money it had borrowed for the first year of federal spending, let alone fund any more. Some people feared the money was being given out too hastily (government departments usually moved very slowly) and so would be wasted when projects collapsed.

Source A: *An anti-Roosevelt cartoon from 1935, suggesting that his 'priming the pump' measures were just wasting money.*

Business opposition

Many people still believed in *laissez faire*, saying relief was not 'the American way', it just encouraged people to be lazy. Many businesses deeply resented the NRA codes and the fines imposed for breaking them. Some chose to work outside the NRA, but lost customers as a result.

Republican opposition

Some Republicans supported the New Deal, but many still supported *laissez faire*. Even more were suspicious of federal control, fearing it was a step towards **communism**, which had taken over in the USSR and which it was believed had many followers in the USA.

Radical opposition

Some opponents of FDR felt he wasn't going far enough. They said he should **nationalise** banks, make stronger laws against big business and introduce social reforms such as pensions and unemployment benefit. Two of these critics had a lot of public support and FDR feared their opposition would damage his reputation, especially as they had supported him in 1932.

Huey Long, Governor and Senator for Louisiana, had made many reforms in that state, taxing the rich to provide work, schools and homes for the poor and unemployed. He criticised the New Deal for not going far enough and in 1935 announced he was going to run for president in the 1936 election. A few months later he was assassinated.

Father Coughlin, a Catholic priest, was famous for his radio talks that called for a fairer society. He was anti-capitalist, but also anti-communist; the talks were said to have an audience of well over 30 million a week. In 1934 he formed the National Union of Social Justice and became more openly critical of FDR's government. He supported Long when he said he would run for president. After Long's assassination he and several other radical opponents supported the candidacy of William Lemke.

Too much power?

One of the biggest worries, though, was that the federal government was becoming too powerful. Some people worried that federal government was taking power away from the states and would keep doing so until states just carried out federal orders.

Others were more worried about the long-term effects of this federal control on the US system of government. It made emergency legislation easy and effective, but it was, they argued, actually unconstitutional. The separation of powers between those who make laws and those who carry them out was part of the Constitution, but some people felt that Roosevelt's executive branch was controlling the legislative branch – Congress. Fears deepened when agencies reached the end of the term set by the emergency legislation and Roosevelt proposed keeping them going.

The Supreme Court Acts

Several groups tried to take cases to the Supreme Court to test the rights of the Alphabet Agencies.

The Supreme Court's first act against the Alphabet Agencies came in what was known as 'the sick chicken case'. In 1934, Schechter Poultry Co, run by the Schechter brothers, was prosecuted for breaking several NRA codes, including selling diseased poultry and setting their prices low to undercut other poultry sellers. They appealed to the Supreme Court, saying the NRA was acting unconstitutionally and as they only sold chickens in one state, it was a state, not a federal issue. On 27 May 1935, the Schechters won. This was just the beginning. During 1935–37 the Supreme Court invalidated more laws passed by Congress than ever before. It overthrew the NRA. It stopped the work of the Federal Farm Board (set up to help farmers with loans and mortgages). It ruled the AAA and several other New Deal Agencies as unconstitutional. One of the few Alphabet Agencies it did not declare illegal was the TVA, because it operated over several states.

Activities

1 a Draw a mind map to show the opposition to the New Deal.

   b Colour code your mind map to show *ideological* reasons (beliefs, values and ideas) for opposing the New Deal, and *financial* reasons.

   c What makes **b** difficult to do?

2 Write a sentence or two to explain how each of the following people might feel on hearing of the Supreme Court decision on the Schechter case:

   a President Roosevelt

   b the Schechters' customers

   c small businesses that are NRA members.

3 Research Dr Francis Townsend. How did he oppose the New Deal?

Source B: *The Schechter brothers celebrate the news of their Supreme Court victory. It was the first ruling against an Alphabet Agency.*

examzone
Top tip!

It is important to remember which bit of the US government is which, and you won't have the diagram on page 7 of this book to help you in the exam. Try making up a memory aid to remind you of each part, for example, laws from **C**ongress = **S**enate + House of **R**epresentatives could be local **c**limate = **s**now + **r**ain.

Extent of recovery, 1935

> **Learning objectives**
>
> In this chapter you will learn about:
> ● how effective the New Deal had been by 1935.

In 1935, Roosevelt started the wave of laws that is often called the Second New Deal. By then, the first New Deal faced opposition from many sides. The Supreme Court was even hearing cases to call more than one New Deal agency 'unconstitutional'. So, had the first New Deal failed in its aim of stopping the downward spiral of the Depression by stabilising finance and providing employment and relief for those in need?

Stabilising finance

When Roosevelt took over in 1933, he temporarily closed the banks because they were in so much difficulty. Once the banks re-opened after the financial inspections, there was no run on the banks. People began to save again. The banks, in their turn, were happier to allow loans and mortgages to run for longer, rather than demanding repayment.

Roosevelt had raised taxes on people and goods, to help pay for the New Deal. In 1932 and 1933, the total tax bill was $1.9bn a year. In 1934, it was $2.9 billion. This, and money saved on government spending (including wages), did not cover New Deal spending, but it kept the government debt manageable.

Providing employment

As the table in Source B shows, the various employment projects halted the rapid rise in the unemployment rate and the rate was dropping by 1935. However, many people complained that the employment was temporary, and certainly most of it was unskilled.

Providing relief

Some agencies helped people to extend their loans so they did not become homeless. Others provided some money, to pay the rent or buy food. Soup kitchens were still busy every day. But the humiliations of claiming relief were still there. Because so many people needed help, this was the area where it was hardest to make a difference.

Estimates show 12 or 13 million unemployed last March. Of these, in the short space of a few months, at least 6 million have been given employment ... We have spent greater sums in co-operation with the states for work relief and home relief than ever before ... We have set up systems for farm and home credit relief in every one of the 3,100 counties of the United States and every day that passes they save homes and farms for hundreds of families.

Source A: *From Roosevelt's fireside chat for 22 October 1933.*

Year	Number unemployed	% of the total workforce
1931	8,020,000	15.9
1932	12,060,000	23.6
1933	12,830,000	24.9
1934	11,340,000	21.7
1935	10,610,000	20

Federal spending in billions of dollars		
Year	Total	Non-military
1931	3.5	2.1
1932	4.7	3.2
1933	4.7	3.2
1934	6.7	5.2
1935	6.5	4.8

Source B: *US government statistics: employment and federal spending, 1931–34.*

Dear Mr President: This is just to tell you that everything is all right now. The man you sent found our house all right, and we went down to the bank with him and the mortgage can go on for a while longer. You remember I wrote you about losing the furniture too. Well, your man got it back for us. I never heard of a President like you.

Source C: *From a letter written to Roosevelt by an elderly couple in the summer of 1933.*

VANITY FAIR

SEPTEMBER 1934
PRICE 35 CENTS
© THE CONDE NAST
PUBLICATIONS, INC.

Source E: *The cover of a US magazine from 1934, showing the NRA eagle rescuing Uncle Sam.*

I finally went on relief. The interview was utterly ridiculous and humiliating. There were questions like: Where's your family? I had sent my wife and child to her folks in Ohio, where they could live more simply. Why should anybody give you money? Why should anybody give you a place to sleep? What sort of friends? This went on for half an hour. I did get certified some time later. I think they paid $9 a month. I came away feeling I didn't have any business living any more.

Source D: *From an interview with Ward James, an editor, who lost his job in 1935.*

Activities

1 Draw two graphs showing the information in Source B.

2 **a** Draw up a table with two columns, headed, 'Successes of the New Deal' and 'Problems of the New Deal'. Check through pages 58–65, and list in your table all the things you think are successes and problems.

   b Overall, does your table suggest the New Deal was a success or a failure?

3 Question 2 has taken you through the stages of answering a judgement question, like question 3 in the exam.

   Use your table to answer this question.

   Was the New Deal a success by 1935?

   Explain your answer. You may use the following information to help you with your answer:

   ● the first 100 days
   ● the Alphabet Agencies
   ● opposition, including the Supreme Court
   ● unemployment.

examzone
Build better answers

Explain the effects of the New Deal on the USA by 1935. **(8 marks)**

The examination will always have questions on the effects of an event – like this one.

■ **A basic answer (level 1)** would give one or two effects without any information to support them.

● **A good answer (level 2)** would give detailed information to illustrate each effect. (For example, ... *unemployment stopped going up rapidly, at first it stuck at about 12m, and then it began to go down. People were helped in other ways, too. There are letters to Roosevelt about government officials extending mortgages on homes and so on.*)

▲ **A better answer (level 3)** would explain why each reason was important. (For example, ... *Unemployment dropping from 12m to 11m was important. It showed people that the Depression could be halted, that the USA could get back to much lower unemployment.*)

▲ **An excellent answer (top marks)** would show links between effects. (For example, *The New Deal began to reverse various parts of the Depression's downward spiral. It slowed and then began to reduce unemployment. Banks were stabilised, so people stopped panicking about their money and the various Loan Acts helped people do things like extend their loans. All this built confidence.*)

The Second New Deal

Learning objectives

In this chapter you will learn about:
● the policies of the Second New Deal.

In January 1935, Roosevelt's annual message to Congress made it clear he wanted the temporary federal/state co-operation that was set up in 1933 to continue. Despite his stress on 'co-operation', this confirmed the fears of many opponents that this meant permanent federal control of the states' affairs. Roosevelt talked of setting up a permanent social-security system to provide unemployment and sickness benefits and old-age pensions. He also proposed federal funding of low-cost housing and an agency to deal with the problems of those made homeless in the Dust Bowl (see page 52).

Source A: *A government information poster from 1935, explaining how to join the social-security scheme.*

New Alphabet Agencies

In April 1935, the Emergency Relief Appropriation Act set up the Works Progress Administration (WPA) to fund various work projects. The WPA funded adult-education classes, acting groups and furniture-building workshops as well as public building works. On 1 May, the Resettlement Act set up the Resettlement Administration (RA) to build new communities for the homeless from cities and the countryside. The National Labor Relations Act (or Wagner Act) was passed in July 1935 and gave all workers the legal right to form trade unions and take strike action. It would give non-skilled workers proper representation and it was hoped it would be one of the reforms that would prevent the suffering of the Depression from happening again. Unions quickly took advantage, with the Congress of Industrial Organisations (CIO), led by John L. Lewis, being notably successful in gaining union recognition due to their sit-in strikes at the General Motors car plant at Flint, Michigan in 1935–6.

In 1936, on the back of his reform programme and the support it gathered, Roosevelt was re-elected.

Taking on the Supreme Court

Roosevelt's re-election, combined with the number of Democrats in Congress who supported him, gave him confidence to carry on with his reforms. It also gave him confidence to tackle the Supreme Court, which had become increasingly difficult about the Alphabet Agencies. On 27 May, it struck its first blow against federal control by deciding the NRA was unconstitutional (see page 61). It passed a similar ruling against the Agricultural Adjustment Agency in January 1936. Several smaller agencies followed.

So, in 1937, Roosevelt began a campaign to 'pack' the Supreme Court – to get judges into it who favoured the New Deal. He proposed to add a new judge for every judge over the age of 70 who had not retired (six out of nine at the time). This shocked many Americans as it shifted the balance of power in the constitution to the President (see page 7). Even his Vice-President was against it.

Roosevelt accused the Supreme Court in a fireside chat as 'reading into the Constitution words and implications that are not there and were never intended to be there.' Still, there was little support for the plan. In the end, Roosevelt didn't need it. Deaths and retirements amongst the judges allowed Roosevelt to nominate new judges more likely to support the New Deal. This, together with the threat, was enough. The Supreme Court now made several decisions supporting the WPA, the RA and the Wagner Act.

Dealing with the Dust Bowl

Conditions worsened in the Dust Bowl in 1935–36. Black blizzards blew harder, for longer, more often. In 1936, rain came – heavy rain that flooded many places and swept away much remaining topsoil. Hundreds of thousands of people had left to become migrant workers in other states. They travelled around, by car or on foot, following the seasonal crops. Many went to California, which found it hard to cope with the numbers of migrants they called 'Oakies' (even though only about 20% came from Oklahoma). The Farm Security Administration (FSA), which was part of the RA, set up more permanent camps and made sure they were supplied with food after 1937.

Further legislation

In 1935, the Soil Conservancy Service was set up to encourage farmers to farm more efficiently using crop rotation and fertilisers, to prevent the Dust Bowl spreading and, eventually, to re-farm it. A new AAA was set up to work along much the same lines as the old one. The 1937 Federal Housing Act set the Federal Housing Administration (FHA) to work on slum clearance and building homes for low-income families. All these agencies were careful to work by approving and funding locally run projects, to avoid accusations of federal takeovers.

A New Deal for all?

The Depression had also, for the first time, brought many white Americans down to the level of poverty endured by black people, which brought their plight to centre stage. Roosevelt's wife, Eleanor, campaigned for the benefits of the New Deal to be applied to blacks and whites equally and helped boost the status of the civil rights movement.

Activities

1 Write a paragraph to explain why you think Source B became the photo that summed up the Dust Bowl and the Depression for so many people.

2 Draw a diagram to show how the following are linked: Roosevelt's speech to Congress in January 1935, the Supreme Court's anti-New Deal rulings, Roosevelt's attempt to 'pack' the Supreme Court, the Supreme Court's pro-New Deal rulings. Use a solid line to show links you are sure about and a dotted line to show possible links.

Source B: *A photograph taken in 1936 by Dorothea Lange, an RA photographer. For many people this woman, Florence Owens Thompson, a migrant worker, is the face of the Dust Bowl and the Depression.*

Extent of recovery, 1941

> ## Learning objectives
>
> In this chapter you will learn about:
> ● how effective the New Deal had been by 1941.

The economy generally improved between 1935 and 1941, but not without hiccups. Banks were stable and under government control. People trusted them again. The Alphabet Agencies were funding employment and relief, although this was patchy and some states worked harder at proposing projects than others, so got more funding.

Providing employment

The WPA (see page 68) spent about $8.5 billion on projects that employed over 8.5 million people. It was town-based and the work ranged from teaching, to building schools, to performing plays. It also set up training schemes to give the unemployed wider skills. The CCC (see page 61) spent about $1.2 billion on rural projects.

Providing relief

From 1935 to 1941, the FSA (see page 61) spent $128 million in relief. The Social Security Act of 1935 didn't start collecting money, or paying it out, until 1937. It took that long to give all those eligible (full-time workers not working for the government or in farming) a social security number. The FHA (see page 61) had built over 120,000 'family units' on slum clearance land by 1941, providing homes for people on low incomes.

1938: a bad year

From the autumn of 1937, all through 1938, the economy worsened in what became known as the 'Roosevelt Recession'. Industrial production fell and unemployment rose. The 1935 Labour Relations Act had stopped employers from banning unions. Union membership had grown and now they organised strikes. The government had cut its spending for the first time, breaking Roosevelt's normal policy of not worrying about balancing the federal budget. However, before things could get worse, the Second World War intervened.

The Second World War

The Second World War began on 3 September 1939. The USA did not enter the war until December 1941, but did supply the Allies with weapons and food from the start. So war production began, creating more and more jobs. As employment rose, so industrial disputes stopped and production started to rise again.

In March 1941 the Lend-Lease Act allowed the US government to provide all help to the Allies 'short of actual war'. More jobs were created in industry, food production and, as the US prepared to join the war, the armed services. By December 1941, when the US entered the war, the economy had improved and continued to do so as war production continued.

Year	Number unemployed	% of all those working
1935	10,610,000	20.1
1936	9,030,000	16.9
1937	7,700,000	14.3
1938	10,390,000	19.0
1939	9,480,000	17.2
1940	8,120,000	14.6
1941	5,560,000	9.9

Source A: *US government statistics: unemployment, 1935–41.*

Federal spending in billions of dollars		
Year	**Total**	**Non-military**
1935	6.5	4.8
1936	8.5	6.6
1937	7.8	5.7
1938	6.8	4.6
1939	8.9	6.5
1940	9.1	6.2
1941	13.3	5.9

Source B: *US government statistics: federal spending, 1935–41.*

Activities

1 Compare Source C below with Source D on page 51. They show the same Hooverville in 1933 and 1939. If a local newspaper had asked for letters saying whether the New Deal was working or not, what do you think someone who lived here would have said? Write the letter.

2 As a class or a group, draw up a balance sheet of successes and failures for the New Deal from 1935 to 1941. Overall, how had it done?

3 Think about your answer to the same question for 1933–35. How did the New Deal do over the whole period? Write a paragraph to sum up your view.

examzone
Top tip!

When you consider the success or failure of policies, be careful to remember that no policy affects everyone in any country in the same way. Always try, in your answer, to consider how a policy would affect different types of people.

Source C: *The same Hooverville in Seattle as shown on page 51, this time photographed in 1939. Soon after, many of the people who lived there went to work in aircraft factories and shipyards set up for war production.*

Roosevelt's role

> **Learning objectives**
>
> In this chapter you will learn about:
> ● Roosevelt's role in recovery.

Historians have different views on Roosevelt's role in recovery. Their views range from 'not that important' to 'vital' – with many shades of opinion in between.

Not that important?

Some historians point out that Hoover was beginning, slowly and unwillingly, to abandon *laissez faire* before Roosevelt was elected (see page 48). They suggest that Hoover might have brought in a version of the New Deal if he had been elected. They believe that politicians would have had to introduce some form of New Deal anyway; it just happened that Roosevelt was president when the shift took place.

Vital?

The other argument is that the Depression was spiralling downhill so fast that it needed quick action to stop it. Hoover would not have moved quickly enough. Roosevelt had worked out what needed to happen so, as soon as he was elected, he went to Congress and suggested working together on emergency legislation. He was not afraid of enlarging federal control to cope with the emergency of the Depression. Nor was he afraid of not 'balancing the budget'. (A balanced budget takes as much money in taxes as the government spends, so it does not have to borrow money.) Roosevelt spent what he believed he needed to, and borrowed money to pay for it. They point out that one of the biggest problems in the Depression was people's lack of confidence and that Roosevelt, with his fireside chats and fatherly manner, made people feel confident.

Re-election

In 1940, there was another presidential election. It was traditional that presidents only served two terms. Roosevelt ran for re-election. He was careful to send a message to the Democratic Convention selecting the candidate to say he would not stand unless 'drafted' (told to by the convention). Just as with the New Deal Agencies, he was breaking the rules, but getting other people to agree to him doing so. He was 'drafted'. He won by 38 states to 10. For three elections running, Americans had voted for him in such large numbers that his opponent never stood a chance. Millions of them had benefited from the New Deal's jobs and financial help.

I think Roosevelt is the biggest-hearted man we ever had in the White House. He can speak his thoughts the clearest of any man I ever heard. He's spoken very few words over the radio that I haven't listened to. It's the first time I can remember a president saying, 'I'm interested in, and going to do something for, the working man.' He made a lot of us feel better, even when there wasn't much to eat in our homes.

Source A: *Said by a mill worker in a newspaper interview in 1936.*

> **Did you know?**
>
> After his break with tradition, Roosevelt was the only US president to be elected for more than two terms. In 1947 the 22nd Amendment to the Constitution was passed, saying that no president could serve more than two terms.

> **Exam-style question**
>
> **Explain the effects of the New Deal on people who were unemployed in the Depression.** (8 marks)

Activities

1   Draw up a mind map of all Roosevelt's main policies and actions from the election of 1932 through to 1941. Put Roosevelt in the middle, and show all the positive things above Roosevelt, and all the negative things below him.

2   Add the following consequences of the New Deal to your mind map, and draw lines connecting the relevant policies to the consequences.

   ● Unemployment fell

   ● The banking system recovered

   ● More help for the unemployed and their families

   ● The National Debt rose

3   Use your mind map as a plan to answer this question. *Was the New Deal a complete success in dealing with the problems of the Depression?*

   Use the bullet points above to help you.

Source B: *A poster from the 1940 presidential election campaign.*

Build better answers

Exam question: Was Roosevelt a success in helping the USA recover from the Depression? Explain your answer.
You may use the following to help you:
● **New Deal policies**
● **restoration of confidence**
You must also include information of your own.

(16 marks)

This question is about *causation*.

■   **A basic answer (level 1)** makes a simple generalisation about causes.

●   **A good answer (level 2)** agrees and/or disagrees with the proposition in the question but does not explain the impact of other suggested consequences (for example *… the New Deal policies show that he was a success and his fireside chats were a big builder of confidence. But you also have to think that the Second World War played a big part in the recovery too*). A more complete answer will examine more than two causes.

▲   **A better answer (level 3)** will explain the causes discussed.

▲   **An excellent answer (level 4)** will prioritise the causes, or see links between them (for example, … *Right at the start his fireside chats built confidence and got people to trust the banks again because they trusted him and he took the banks under federal control. The New Deal policies were his idea and they worked. They provided people with work and relief and the fact that the government was giving this help, on an organised, country-wide level through the Alphabet Agencies was vital to economic improvement and built confidence in people. But he didn't start the Second World War, which was a big factor in pulling people out of the 1938 economic dip. This doesn't mean he wasn't a success though, because his ideas we hugely helpful – people must have thought he was a success – he got re-elected for a third time, even though you were supposed only to get re-elected twice…..*).

Make sure you write accurately – there are 4 extra marks available for spelling, grammar and punctuation in these questions.

74

In the Unit 2 exam, you will have to answer six questions: Question 1(a), (b), (c) and (d); either Question 2(a) or Question 2(b); and either Question 3(a) or Question 3(b). You have only 1 hour and 15 minutes to answer these questions.

Here we are going to look at Question 3. You should allow about 25 minutes for this question. In addition to the 16 marks available for this question, there are 4 additional marks available for spelling, punctuation and grammar. Make sure you leave some time at the end to check these aspects of your answer.

examzone

Build better answers

Question 3

Tip: Both Question 3(a) and 3(b) will ask you to use your knowledge to make judgements on causes, effects or importance of factors. In the examination, you choose to answer whichever of (a) or (b) you like the most. Do not do both (a) and (b) as the examiners will give you marks for only one of them. Remember that this is the highest-scoring question on the paper and requires a substantial and detailed response. You will be spending around 25 minutes on this answer, so you cannot write at enormous length. However, you should:

- use the examples given in the question and at least one of your own
- provide factual information from the sources on the paper and your own knowledge
- make judgements on the relative importance of the causes, effects or important features.

We are going to pick a causation question and work our way through the levels until we have a high level 4 response.

The question we will use is:

Was his ability to communicate with the American people the main reason why Roosevelt was able to lead the USA out of the Depression?

> You may use the following information to help you with your answer:
> - Roosevelt's speeches and fireside chats
> - the 'Second New Deal'

Student answer

I think the important reasons were the speeches and the fireside chats, and all the jobs that came with re-armament and the Second World War.

Comments

I am afraid that in a 16-mark question requiring extended writing, this isn't going to score many marks! The answer develops two points, one from the examples and one from their own knowledge, so it would be a high level 2. However, it hasn't addressed the question of communication as a main reason, nor has it made a judgement and supported it.

So let's provide that detail. The new parts are in bold.

Student answer	Comments
I think the important reasons were the speeches and the fireside chats, and all the jobs that came with re-armament and the Second World War. **When Roosevelt won the election in 1932, most Americans had no confidence their country could get out of the mess it was in. As soon as he came to power, he made them feel better – he said, 'we have nothing to fear, but fear itself.' But when Europe went to war again in 1939, Roosevelt sold food and weapons to the Allies in a policy called lend-lease, and also built up the US forces, and this all created lots of jobs, and unemployment finally came down.**	Now we are beginning to get some information into our answer and to write some history instead of the generalised comments made in the previous answer. The answer develops two points, so it would score towards the top of level 2. However, although it provides factual support for the two reasons given, it doesn't bring in any new reasons or suggest how important the reasons were. For example, was one reason more important than the others?

So let's do what the examiner wants. We will put the new parts in bold.

I think the speeches and the fireside chats **were important.** When Roosevelt won the election in 1932, most Americans had no confidence their country could get out of the mess it was in. As soon as he came to power, he made them feel better – he said, 'we have nothing to fear, but fear itself.' **However there was opposition to the New Deal from business and the Supreme Court, and unemployment went up in 1938, so this can't have been enough. When** Europe went to war again in 1939, Roosevelt sold food and weapons to the Allies in a policy called lend-lease, and also built up the US forces, and this all created lots of jobs. and all the jobs that came with re-armament and the Second World War. **So the war must have been more important as the New Deal could have failed without it.**	We are getting to a high standard now. The answer has brought in reasons not given in the question (opposition and unemployment in 1938), has looked at a variety of factors and decided that one of them (the Second World War) was more important than the others. We are now at the top of level 3. We just need to show that the reasons are all interlinked to get to level 4.

Now let's introduce that linking by adding the following paragraph at the end of the above answer.

While I think re-armament and the Second World War was the most important thing, it wasn't the only thing. If Roosevelt hadn't been able to convince people, things would not have got better. Without the Alphabet Agencies people would have been in a mess and Roosevelt might not have been re-elected, so they are all part of the answer, but the fireside chats and the two New Deals weren't enough, only the war finally ended the Depression.	Lovely! **Note:** remember that Question 3 is one on which your skills of written communication will be judged and the accuracy of your spelling, punctuation and grammar will be marked. Do your best to write effectively, organise coherently, and spell, punctuate and use grammar with considerable accuracy.

Welcome to examzone

Revising for your exams can be a daunting prospect. Use this section of the book to get ideas, tips and practice to help you prepare as best as you can.

Zone In!

Have you ever become so absorbed in a task that it suddenly feels entirely natural? This is a feeling familiar to many athletes and performers: it's a feeling of being 'in the zone' that helps you focus and achieve your best.

Here are our top tips for getting in the zone with your revision.

● **Understand the exam process** and what revision you need to do. This will give you confidence but also help you to put things into proportion. Use the Planning Zone to create a revision plan.

● **Build your confidence** by using your revision time, not just to revise the information you need to know, but also to practise the skills you need for the examination. Try answering questions in timed conditions so that you're more prepared for writing answers in the exam.

● **Deal with distractions** by making a list of everything that might interfere with your revision and how you can deal with each issue. For example, revise in a room without a television, but plan breaks in your revision so that you can watch your favourite programmes.

● **Share your plan with friends and family** so that they know not to distract you when you want to revise. This will mean you can have more quality time with them when you aren't revising.

● **Keep healthy** by making sure you eat well and exercise, and by getting enough sleep. If your body is not in the right state, your mind won't be either – and staying up late to cram the night before the exam is likely to leave you too tired to do your best.

Planning Zone

The key to success in exams and revision often lies in the right planning, so that you don't leave anything until the last minute. Use these ideas to create your personal revision plan.

First, fill in the dates of your examinations. Check with your teacher when these are if you're not sure. Add in any regular commitments you have. This will help you get a realistic idea of how much time you have to revise.

▼

Know your strengths and weaknesses and assign more time to topics you find difficult – don't be tempted to leave them until the last minute.

▼

Create a revision 'checklist' using the Know Zone lists and use them to check your knowledge and skills.

▼

Now fill in the timetable with sensible revision slots. Chunk your revision into smaller sections to make it more manageable and less daunting. Make sure you give yourself regular breaks and plan in different activities to provide some variety.

▼

Keep to the timetable! Put your plan up somewhere visible so you can refer back to it and check that you are on track.

Know zone

In this zone, you'll find some useful suggestions about how to structure your revision, and checklists to help you test your learning for each of the main topics. You might want to skim-read this before you start your revision planning, as it will help you think about how best to revise the content.

Remember that different people learn in different ways – some remember visually and therefore might want to think about using diagrams and other drawings for their revision, whereas others remember better through sound or through writing things out. Try to think about what works best for you by trying out some of the techniques below.

- **Summaries**: writing a summary of the information in a chapter can be a useful way of making sure you've understood it. But don't just copy it all out. Try to reduce each paragraph to a couple of sentences. Then try to reduce the couple of sentences to a few words!

- **Concept maps**: if you're a visual learner, you may find it easier to take in information by representing it visually. Draw concept maps or other diagrams. They are particularly good to show links, for example you could create a concept map which shows the effects of the New Deal on the Depression. It would involve arrows pointing to such things as 'land losses', 'military losses' etc.

- **Mnemonics**: this is when you take the first letter of a series of words you want to remember and then make a new sentence.

- **Index cards**: write important events and people on index cards then test yourself on why they were important.

- **Timelines**: create a large, visual timeline and annotate it in colour.

- **Quizzes**: let's face it, learning stuff can be dull. Why not make a quiz out of it? Set a friend 20 questions to answer. Make up multiple-choice questions. You might even make up your own exam questions and see if you friend can answer them!

And then when you are ready:

- practice questions – go back through the sample exam questions in this book to see if you can answer them (without cheating!)

- try writing out some of your answers in timed conditions so that you're used to the amount of time you'll have to answer each type of question in the exam.

If you are sitting your exams from 2014 onwards, you will be sitting all your exams together at the end of your course. Make sure you know in which order you are sitting the exams, and prepare for each accordingly – check with your teacher if you're not sure. They are likely to be about a week apart, so make sure you allow plenty of revision time for each before your first exam.

Know Zone Unit 2C Key Topic 1

You should know about the following things. If you can't remember any of them, just look at the page number and re-read that chapter.

You should know about...

How the US economy benefitted from the First World War **(pages 8–9)**

❑ What boosted US economic confidence in the 1920s **(page 9)**

❑ Why the USA refused to join the League of Nations **(pages 10)**

❑ Why the USA began to impose quotas on immigration **(page 11)**

❑ The importance of the Ford motor industry **(pages 12–13)**

❑ How mass production affected industry **(pages 12–13)**

❑ The effect the growth of new industries had on the economy **(pages 14–15)**

❑ The impact hire purchase had on consumers and industry **(pages 14–15)**

❑ What happened in the stock market boom **(pages 16–17)**

❑ What economic problems some older industries had **(page 18)**

❑ Why farmers' prices fell after the First World War **(page 19)**

❑ Why advertising was a powerful tool **(page 20)**

❑ The underlying problems of the boom, including overproduction, lack of credit control and problems in the stock market **(pages 21–3)**

Key people

Do you know why these people or groups are important?

Congress **(page 7)**   Calvin Coolidge **(page 9)**

The Supreme Court **(page 7)**   Henry Ford **(pages 12–13)**

Woodrow Wilson **(page 10)**   Herbert Hoover **(page 14)**

Key events and ideas

Do you know about the events below? Do you know what the key phrases mean? If not, go back to the page and look them up!

Events

The Emergency Tariff Act is passed, May 1921 **(page 10)**

The boom **(pages 14–15)**

Phrases

Laissez faire **(page 9)**

Isolationism **(page 10)**

Trade tariffs **(page 10)**

Mass production **(pages 12–13)**

New industries **(page 14)**

Hire purchase **(page 14)**

Boom cycle **(page 15)**

The stock market **(page 16)**

Buying on the margin **(page 17)**

Test your spelling

Remember that in question 3, the accuracy of your spelling is one element of your answer that will be assessed. Make sure you can spell the key events, ideas and people listed above, and the following terms from this key topic:

agriculture	employment	isolationism
assembly line	hire purchase	legislative
Congress	federal	manufacture
constitution	government	mechanisation
dividend	immigration	standardisation
economy/economic	industry	

You should know about the following things. If you can't remember any of them, just look at the page number and re-read that chapter.

You should know about...

- ☐ The social impact of consumerism **(page 27)**
- ☐ How more leisure time affected peoples' lives **(page 27–8)**
- ☐ Why the entertainment industry grew **(pages 28–9)**
- ☐ What impact the movies had on peoples' lives **(page 28–9)**
- ☐ How and why the role of women changed in the 1920s **(pages 30–1)**
- ☐ What impact the Prohibition had on everyday life **(pages 32–3)**
- ☐ How 'Jim Crow' laws affected life in the South **(page 34)**
- ☐ What effects racism had the USA, including the Ku Klux Klan **(pages 34–7)**
- ☐ How prejudice against immigrants showed itself **(pages 38)**
- ☐ How some states showed religious intolerance **(pages 39)**

Key people

Do you know why these people or groups are important?

The Anti-Saloon League **(page 32)**   Uncle Sam **(page 37)**

Al Capone **(page 32–3)**   Sacco and Vanzetti **(page 38)**

The Ku Klux Klan **(page 37)**   John Scopes **(page 39)**

Test your spelling

Remember that in question 3, the accuracy of your spelling is one element of your answer that will be assessed. Make sure you can spell the key events, ideas and people listed above, and the following terms from this key topic:

advertising	industry
business	prejudice
consumerism	Prohibition
discrimination	racism
immorality	segregation

Key events and ideas

Do you know about the events below? Do you know what the key phrases mean? If not, go back to the page and look them up!

Events

Women's Suffrage, 18 August 1920 **(page 30)**

St Valentine's Day Massacre, 14 February 1929 **(page 33)**

Execution of Sacco and Vanzetti, 23 August 1927 **(page 38)**

Phrases

the Hays Code **(page 29)**

suffrage **(page 30)**

flapper **(page 31)**

Prohibition **(page 32)**

speakeasy **(page 32)**

bootleg alcohol **(page 32)**

Gangsterism **(page 33)**

'Jim Crow' laws **(page 34)**

lynch law **(page 36)**

the Monkey Trial **(page 39)**

Exam Zone

Know Zone Unit 2C Key Topic 3

You should know about the following things. If you can't remember any of them, just look at the page number and re-read that chapter.

80

You should know about...

❏ How rapidly share prices fell during the Wall Street Crash **(page 43)**

❏ How the Wall Street Crash affected banks and businesses **(page 44)**

❏ How the Wall Street Crash affected savers **(page 44)**

❏ How the Depression affected the USA **(pages 46–51)**

❏ What action the government took to try to stop the Depression **(pages 48–9)**

❏ Why the government became unpopular **(pages 54–5)**

Key events and ideas

Do you know about the events below? Do you know what the key phrases mean? If not, go back to the page and look them up!

Events

the Wall Street Crash October 1929 **(page 44)**

Phrases

soup kitchen **(page 47)**

rugged individualism **(page 48)**

shanty town **(page 50)**

Hooverville **(page 50–51)**

flophouse **(page 52)**

the Dust Bowl **(page 52)**

Key people

Do you know why these people or groups are important?

Herbert Hoover **(page 48)**

POUR **(page 48)**

The Reconstruction Finance Corporation **(page 49)**

The Bonus Army **(page 55)**

Test your spelling

Remember that in question 3, the accuracy of your spelling is one element of your answer that will be assessed. Make sure you can spell the key events, ideas and people listed above, and the following terms from this key topic:

bankrupt/bankruptcy

economic

federal

laissez faire

Republican

tariff

You should know about the following things. If you can't remember any of them, just look at the page number and re-read that chapter.

You should know about...

❑ What Roosevelt's aims were for the early years of the New Deal **(page 59)**

❑ What was different about the Hundred Days **(page 60–1)**

❑ What the New Deal did to solve the problems in finance **(pages 60–1)**

❑ What the New Deal did to solve the problems of industry **(pages 60–2)**

❑ What the New Deal did to solve the problems of agriculture **(pages 60–2)**

❑ What the New Deal did to solve the problems of unemployed **(pages 60–2)**

❑ How the Alphabet Agencies worked with states and local government to help the poor and unemployed **(pages 62–3)**

❑ Why people criticised the New Deal **(pages 64–5)**

❑ Why the Supreme Court ruled against some Alphabet Agencies **(page 65)**

❑ How effective the New Deal had been by 1935 **(pages 66–7)**

❑ What the aims and achievements of the Second New Deal **(pages 68–9)**

❑ How Roosevelt tried to control the Supreme Court **(page 68)**

❑ How effective the New Deal had been by 1941 **(pages 70–1)**

❑ The role of Roosevelt in recovery **(pages 72–3)**

Key events and ideas

Do you know about the events below? Do you know what the key phrases mean? If not, go back to the page and look them up!

Events

The Hundred Days, 9 March–16 June 1933 **(pages 60–1)**

Phrases

fireside chats **(page 59)**

Alphabet Agencies **(page 50)**

priming the pump **(page 62)**

The Schechter brothers and the 'sick chicken case' **(page 65)**

Key people

Do you know why these people or groups are important?

Franklin D Roosevelt **(page 59)**

The Tennessee Valley Authority (TVA) **(pages 61, 62, 65)**

The Civilian Conservation Corps (CCC) **(pages 60–1)**

Huey Long **(page 64)**

Father Coughlin **(page 64)**

The Schechter brothers **(page 65)**

Test your spelling

Remember that in questions 2 and 3, the accuracy of your spelling is one element of your answer that will be assessed. Make sure you can spell the key events, ideas and people listed above, and the following terms from this key topic:

agricultural

Congress

constitutional (unconstitutional)

federal

legislation

lend-lease

taxation

As the day of the exam gets closer, many students tend to go into panic mode, either working long hours without really giving their brain a chance to absorb information, or giving up and staring blankly at the wall.

Look over your revision notes and go through the checklists to remind yourself of the main areas you need to know about. Don't try to cram in too much new information at the last minute and don't stay up late revising – you'll do better if you get a good night's sleep.

Exam Zone

What to expect in the exam paper

You will have 1 hour and 15 minutes in the examination. There are six questions in the exam paper, and you have to answer all six of them. In Question 1 you don't get a choice – there are four parts to the question (a-d) and you must answer all four. In questions 2 and 3 though, you do get a choice. In each case there are two parts to the question (a and b) and you only answer **one** of them – so either 2a or 2b and either 3a or 3b.

The questions you answer have different numbers of marks available, and we suggest below roughly how long you should spend on each one. The best way to organise your time is to have a few minutes left at the end so you can read through your answers and check your spelling, punctuation and grammar. What you don't want to do, is to run out of time on question 3 – which has the most marks of any question on the paper. One important thing to remember is that the question and answer booklet has lots of lines for each question. This is designed so people with the largest handwriting have room to write a long answer. Don't try to fill all the lines – there are more lines than you will need.

Question 1a is worth 4 marks (about 6 minutes)

It starts with a source written by a historian, and the question asks you what you can learn from the source about something. It could be what you can learn about the impact of an event, or the problems faced, or the reasons for what happened.

Question 1b is worth 6 marks (about 8 minutes)

It asks you to describe something – it could be policies, key features, problems.

Question 1c is worth 8 marks (about 10 minutes)

It asks you to explain the effects of something. Read it carefully, there are two key parts to the question, because, for example, it will ask you to *explain the effects of developments in the car industry* on *the economy in the 1920s*. Make sure you focus on both key parts.

Question 1d is worth 8 marks (about 10 minutes)

This will be a question about causes. You will be asked to *explain why* something happened. Remember, events in history always have more than one cause, and the causes usually link together. Also make sure you explain why the causes you describe led to the event happening.

Question 2 is worth 8 marks (about 12 minutes)

This is a question about change or development, where you have a choice and answer **either** part a **or** part b. Use the extra couple of minutes to think about both questions and decide which to answer. It might help to jot down the main facts you could use in your answer for each possible question. When you know which one is the best for you to do, remember to use facts to support your answer.

Question 3 is worth 16 marks (about 25 minutes)

This question is usually about causes or effects and it is another one where you answer either part a or part b. It is worth almost one third of the marks for the whole paper. So spend a couple of minutes thinking about which is the best one to answer. It is quite different from the other questions in that it gives you some help in listing things you could use in your answer. This is a good hint. You are also told you must include information of your own. Be sure to use the listed examples and add to them from your own knowledge. Try to give as much detail as possible. Your answer for this question will be marked for spelling, punctuation and grammar: there are up to 4 additional marks available for this aspect of your writing.

Meet the exam paper

In this exam you will write all of your answers in the spaces provided on the exam paper. It's important that you use a black pen and that you indicate clearly which questions you have answered where a choice is provided – instructions will be given on the paper. Try to make your handwriting as legible as possible.

Print your surname here, and your other names afterwards. This is an additional safeguard to ensure that the exam board awards the marks to the right candidate.

Here you fill in the school's exam number.

The Unit 2 exam lasts 1 hour 15 minutes. Plan your time accordingly.

Make sure that you understand exactly which questions from which sections you should attempt.

Here you fill in your personal exam number. Take care to write it accurately.

In this box, the examiner will write the total marks you have achieved in the exam paper.

Don't feel that you have to fill the answer space provided. Everybody's handwriting varies, so a long answer from you may take up as much space as a short answer from someone else.

Remember that in question 3 your spelling, punctuation and grammar will be assessed, as well as the quality of your written communication. Take time to check your spelling, punctuation and grammar and to make sure that you have expressed yourself clearly.

Write your name here

Surname

Other names

**Pearson
Edexcel GCSE**

Centre Number

Candidate Number

History A (The Making of the Modern World)
Unit 2: Modern World Depth Study
Option 2C: The USA, 1919–41

Sample Assessment Material for 2013
Time: 1 hour 15 minutes

Paper Reference
5HA02/2C

You do not need any other materials.

Total Marks

Instructions

- Use **black** ink or ball-point pen.
- **Fill in the boxes** at the top of this page with your name, centre number and candidate number.
- Answer **six** questions (1(a), (b), (c), (d), 2(a) **OR** 2(b), 3(a) **OR** 3(b)).
- Answer the questions in the spaces provided
  – there may be more space than you need.

Information

- The total mark for this paper is 54.
- The marks for **each** question are shown in brackets
  – use this as a guide as to how much time to spend on each question.
- Questions labelled with an **asterisk** (*) are ones where the quality of your written communication will be assessed.
- The marks available for spelling, punctuation and grammar are clearly indicated.

Advice

- Read each question carefully before you start to answer it.
- Keep an eye on the time.
- Check your answers if you have time at the end.

S42896A
©2013 Pearson Education Ltd.
Edexcel GCSE in History A

Sample Assessment Materials

Turn over ▶

© Pearson Education Ltd 2013 71

PEARSON

The USA, 1919-41

Answer Questions 1(a) to (d), then Question 2(a) OR 2(b) and then Question 3(a) OR 3(b).

Question 1 – you must answer all parts of this question.

Study Source A.

Source A: From a history of the USA 1919-41, published in 1998.

> The First World War helped the US economy in several ways. Throughout the war there was a one-way trade with Europe. Money poured into the USA for food, raw materials and munitions. The USA took over European overseas markets and many industries became more successful than their European competitors. The war also saw advances in technology such as mechanisation and new materials like plastics.

(a) What can you learn from Source A about the impact of the First World War on the economy of the USA?

(4)

You need to answer Questions 1, 2 and 3. You should answer all parts of Question 1, but for Question 2 and Question 3, you should answer either (a) or (b).

Question 1a
When you answer you should always say what the source tells you, and give a reason for it. A good answer to the question above is: *It tells me the war was good for the American economy.* [what it tells you] *The USA was able to take over the European overseas markets and make money* [the reason].

The number of marks available for each question is given on the right.

(b) Describe the key features of the opposition to Roosevelt's New Deal in the period 1933–36.

(6)

Question 1b
A good answer will make more than one point (the question says **features**) and support or explain each point with some detail you can remember.

(c) Explain the effects that developments in the car industry had on the US economy and society in the 1920s.

(8)

Question 1c
The question says **effects** so make sure you describe at least two effects, and three if you can. Good answers explain how each effect works, e.g. *because there were so many cars, they needed petrol stations all over the country,* [the effect] *and people got new jobs building them and working in them* [the explanation].

Question 1d

This is a causation question, so make sure your answer has more than one cause, and for each cause you include explain why it was a cause, or how it worked, e.g. *After the war there was less demand for home grown food* [the cause] *which meant the farmers sold less, and their income went down* [the explanation]. If you can, show how the causes you write about were linked together.

(d) Explain why there was a depression in US agriculture in the 1920s.

(8)

Question 2

Your explanation should always include more than one reason or feature. Make sure you support or explain each feature, and if you can explain how the features link together, e.g. *Roosevelt tried to get more people in jobs, so he set up the Civilian Conservation Corps in 1933, which gave jobs to many men who were unemployed and living in Hoovervilles. Now these people had money to spend, so they helped keep shops open, by buying things, and as more goods were being sold, more were made, so the CCC wages helped create other jobs in factories as well.*

Answer EITHER Question 2(a) OR 2(b).

EITHER

2 (a) Explain how the role of women in US society changed in the 1920s.

(8)

OR

2 (b) Explain how Roosevelt tackled the problems of unemployment in the years 1933-41.

(8)

Indicate which question you are answering by marking a cross in the box ⊠. If you change your mind, put a line through the box ⊠ and then indicate your new question with a cross ⊠.

Chosen Question Number: **Question 2(a)** ☐ **Question 2(b)** ☐

Either 2a or 2b

Remember, this is one of the questions where you have a choice. Look at both parts, and decide which one to answer, then make sure you put an x in the right box to show which question you have answered.

This asterisk indicates that in this question the quality of your written communication will be assessed. You should always do your best to write neatly and spell and punctuate properly. It's even more important in this question, because some of the marks are for your spelling, punctuation and grammar.

...part (a) or part (b).

Remember to check your spelling, punctuation and grammar when you see this highlighted.

Answer EITHER Question 3(a) OR 3(b).

Spelling, punctuation and grammar will be assessed in this question.

EITHER

*3 (a) Was the collapse of the banks the most important impact of the Wall Street Crash in the period 1929–33? Explain your answer.

(16)

You may use the following in your answer.

- The collapse of the banks
- The impact on businesses

You must also include information of your own.

OR

*3 (b) Was over-production the main reason for the Wall Street Crash of 1929? Explain your answer.

(16)

You may use the following in your answer.

- Over-production
- Protection

You must also include information of your own.

(Total for spelling, punctuation and grammar = 4 marks)
(Total for Question 3 = 20 marks)

Indicate which question you are answering by marking a cross in the box ☒. If you change your mind, put a line through the box ☒ and then indicate your new question with a cross ☒.

Chosen Question Number: **Question 3(a)** ☐   **Question 3(b)** ☐

....
....
....
....

The live question paper will contain three further pages of lines.

TOTAL FOR PAPER = 54 MARKS

...essment Materials   © Pearson Education Ltd 2013   77

Always remember the marks
Use your time wisely. This question is worth 16 marks, one third of all the marks for this exam.

Make sure you put an x in the correct box to show which question you have answered.

Question 3
This question asks you to make a judgement – *was it the most important* impact, or, *was it the main reason.* You also get some help, in that you get a list of impacts or reasons. However, the question also says: *You must also include information of your own.* A good answer must do three things. First, show the examiner you understand a number of reasons. Second, make sure you focus on which was the *most important* impact or the *main* reason. To do this you need to clearly explain several impacts or reasons and explain your judgement. Don't forget to use information of your own in your answer.

Be careful
You should always do your best to write neatly, and spell and punctuate properly. It's even more important in this question, because some of the marks are for the quality of your...

Zone Out

This section provides answers to the most common questions students have about what happens after they complete their exams. For more information, visit www.examzone.co.uk.

When will my results be published?

Results for GCSE examinations are issued on the third Thursday in August.

Can I get my results online?

Visit www.resultsplusdirect.co.uk, where you will find detailed student results information including the `Edexcel Gradeometer' which demonstrates how close you were to the nearest grade boundary.

I haven't done as well as I expected. What can I do now?

First of all, talk to your teacher. After all the teaching that you have had, and the tests and internal examinations you have done, he/she is the person who best knows what grade you are capable of achieving. Take your results slip to your subject teacher, and go through the information on it in detail. If you both think that there is something wrong with the result, the school or college can apply to see your completed examination paper and then, if necessary, ask for a re-mark immediately.

Can I have a re-mark of my examination paper?

Yes, this is possible, but remember only your school or college can apply for a re-mark, not you or your parents/carers. First of all you should consider carefully whether or not to ask your school or college to make a request for a re-mark. It is worth knowing that very few re-marks result in a change to a grade, simply because a re-mark request has shown that the original marking was accurate. Check the closing date for re-marking requests with your Examinations Officer.

Bear in mind that there is no guarantee that your grades will go up if your papers are re-marked. The original mark can be confirmed or lowered, as well as raised, as a result of a re-mark.

Glossary

Term	Definition
Alphabet Agencies	The name given to a group of federal bodies established as part of the New Deal. Most were known by their three-letter acronyms (see page 89).
assembly line	A system where workers all working on the same product wait in a particular place in the factory to do their part of the job while the thing they are putting together (for example, a car) moves from person to person on rails or a conveyor belt.
Congress	The part of the US government that makes the laws, consisting of the House of Representatives and the Senate (see page 7).
communism	A system where everyone is equal, the state owns everything and provides everything that people need.
Constitution	A constitution is the rules for running a country or organisation. It is Constitution when referring to a particular one, for example 'The US Constitution'.
dividend	The share of the profit of a company that is paid to its shareholders, usually yearly.
division of labour	Splitting a job up into several stages, with a different person working on each stage.
emigrate	Leave a country to live somewhere else.
evolution	The theory of evolution states that living things 'evolve' – they change and adapt to their situation. New types of living things evolve from earlier types, they do not just come into being.
executive	To do with carrying out laws.
Federal	Central (used here to refer to central government).
hire purchase	Buying something by paying a small part of the price at first, then paying of the rest of the price in regular payments – so hiring what you have bought until you have paid for it fully.
immigration	Coming to a country to live there.
isolationism	The policy of not becoming involved in the affairs of other countries.
judicial	To do with enforcing laws and punishing crime.
Ku Klux Klan	A racist group in the USA that wanted all Americans to be white, Anglo-Saxon and Protestant. They persecuted people of any other race or religion.
laissez faire	The policy of not interfering in the way people run their business and not providing welfare or care for those who are poor or have other social problems.
legislative	To do with making laws.
mass production	Making goods that have standardised parts (for example, the same sized bolts) to make them quicker and cheaper to assemble.
Prohibition	The period in the USA from 1920–33 when it was illegal to make, sell, or transport alcohol in the USA.
nationalise	The act of taking a major industry into state ownership from the private sector.
shanty towns	Temporary towns where the houses are small, made from cheap materials and usually have no services (such as drains and electricity).

Term	Definition
sharecropper	A farmworker paid not in wages but a share of the harvest.
shares	Where people buy a share in a company by giving the company money – the number of shares they have depends on the money they give. They then get a dividend from the company profits.
speakeasy	A place where you could buy illegal alcohol during Prohibition.
standardisation	Making things the same.
stock market	Where shares are bought and sold.
suffrage	The right to vote.
unions	Groups of workers joining together to protect their interests.
xenophobia	A fear of foreigners.

Agencies	
AAA	Agricultural Adjustment Administration, 1933–35: gave subsidies to farmers to grow less to push prices up, also bought up surplus.
CCC	Civilian Conservation Corps, 1933–42: took men (at first only 17–23 years old) to work on land conservation, living in big, army-run camps.
CWA	Civil Works Administration 1933–34: organised public building works.
FCA	Farm Credit Administration 1933, still running: lent money to farmers who needed help with loans.
FDIC	Federal Deposit Insurance Corporation, 1933, still running: guaranteed savings in federal approved banks.
FHA	Federal Housing Administration: 1934, still running, helps to provide low-cost housing, slum clearance.
FSA	Farm Security Administration 1934–46: part of the RA that carried on after the RA stopped in 1936.
NRA	National Recovery Administration 1933–35: set codes to regulate working conditions and prices for businesses that joined.
PWA	Public Works Administration set up in 1933 with a fixed budget to spend on public works.
RA	Resettlement Administration, 1935–1936, resettled the homeless in 'new towns'.
TVA	Tennessee Valley Authority, 1933, still running: runs land development in the Tennessee Valley, over seven states.
WPA	Works Progress Administration: 1935–43: gave funding for many smaller projects as well as public works. It also provided training in many kinds of jobs.

Published by Pearson Education Limited, Edinburgh Gate, Harlow, Essex, CM20 2JE.

www.pearsonschoolsandfecolleges.co.uk

Copies of official specifications for all Edexcel qualifications may be found on the Edexcel website: www.edexcel.com

Text © Pearson Education Limited 2013
Typeset by HL Studios, Long Hanborough, Oxford
Illustrated by Peter Bull Studio
Cover images: *Front:* **Corbis:** Minnesota Historical Society
All other images © Pearson Education

The rights of Jane Shuter to be identified as authors of this work have been asserted by her in accordance with the Copyright, Designs and Patents Act 1988.

First published 2013

16 15 14
10 9 8 7 6 5 4 3 2

British Library Cataloguing in Publication Data
A catalogue record for this book is available from the British Library

ISBN 978 1 446 92408 2

Printed in Italy by Lego S.p.A

Acknowledgements

The author and publisher would like to thank the following individuals and organisations for permission to reproduce photographs:

(Key: b-bottom; c-centre; l-left; r-right; t-top)
Alamy Images: Image Asset Management Ltd. 43; **Bridgeman Art Library Ltd:** 19; **Corbis:** Bettmann 6, 47, 48, 53, 58, 60, 63, David J & Janice L Frent 30, 37, Hulton-Deutsch Collection 33l, Museum of History and Industry 71, Webster & Stevens Collection 42, 51; **Getty Images:** Hulton Archive 11, Popperfoto 36; **Mary Evans Picture Library:** 15, 27; **TopFoto:** 29, 55, Granger Collection 9, 13, 20, 21, 22, 26, 31, 33r, 35, 39, 45, 54, 64, 65, 67, 68, 69, 73, Roger-Viollet 38

We are grateful to the following for permission to reproduce copyright material:

Tables
Source D, page 43 from *The Great Crash 1929* ISBN-13: 978-0141038254 Penguin (John Kenneth Galbraith) p149, 29 Oct 2009, Penguin Books Ltd

Text
Source C, page 9 from *Alistair Cooke's America* ISBN-13: 978-0465018826 Penguin (Alistair Cooke) 2 Oct 2008, Penguin Books Ltd and Palazzo Editions Ltd; Source E, page 10 from http://history.state.gov/milestones/1921-1936/Protectionism, Office of the Historian, Bureau of Public Affairs, United States Department of State; Source A, page 12 from *My Life and Work - An Autobiography of Henry Ford* ISBN-13: 978-0979311987, BN Publishing (Henry Ford) 28 Jan 2009, www.bnpublishing.com; Source B, page 12 from *Alistair Cooke's America* ISBN-13: 978-0465018826Penguin (Alistair Cooke) 2 Oct 2008, Penguin Books Ltd and Palazzo Editions Ltd; Source A page 14 from *The Free and the Unfree: New History of the United States* ISBN-13: 978-0140165401 Penguin Books Ltd (Peter N Carroll and David W Nobel) 26 Mar 1992, From THE FREE AND THE UNFREE by Peter N. Carroll and David W. Noble, copyright (c) 1977,1988, 2001 by Peter N. Carroll and David W. Noble. Used by permission of Viking Penguin, a division of Penguin Group (USA) LLC; Source C, page 22 from *Historical Dictionary of the Great Depression, 1929-1940* ISBN-13: 978-0313306181 Greenwood Press (James Olsen) p4, 1 Sep 2001, Historical dictionary of the Great Depression, 1929-1940 by OLSON, JAMES Reproduced with permission of GREENWOOD PUBLISHING GROUP in the format Republish in a book via Copyright Clearance Center; Source A, page 28 from *The 1920s (American Popular Culture Through History)* ISBN-13: 978-0313361630 Greenwood Publishing Group (Kathleen Morgan

Drowne & Patrick Huber) p.160, 1 Jan 2004, 1920's by DROWNE, KATHLEEN Reproduced with permission of GREENWOOD PUBLISHING GROUP, INC. in the; format Republish in a book via Copyright Clearance Center; Source B on page 28 from *City Games The Evolution of American Urban Society and the Rise of Sports* 978-0-252-06216-2 University of Illinois Press (Steven A. Riess), From City Games: The Evolution of American Urban Society and the Rise of Sports by Steven A. Riess. Copyright 1989 by the Board of Trustees by the University of Illinois. Used with permission of the University of Illinois Press.; Article on page 28 from *'Prosperity's Child: Some Thoughts on the Flapper by Kenneth A Yellis, University of Rochester 1969. Prosperity's child: the Flapper, Kenneth A Yellis, American Quarterly, Vol 21 No 1 Spring 1969* , Johns Hopkins University Press, Yellis, Kenneth A. "Prosperity's Child: Some Thoughts on the Flapper." American Quarterly 21:1 (1969), 44-64. © 1969 Trustees of the University of Pennsylvania. Reprinted with permission of Johns Hopkins University Press; Extract SourceA .20 from *Black History for Beginners* ISBN 978-1934389195 For Beginners (Denise Dennis 1984); Poetry on page 31 from *Originally from 'The Weary Blues' 1926 : The Collected Poems of Langston Hughes* ISBN-13: 978-0826213419 Alfred Knopf by permission of David Higham Associates (Langston Hughes 2002); Source A, page 36 from *Imagery of Lynching: Black Men, White Women, and the Mob, Dora Apel, Rutgers University Press, 2004, ISBN 978-0813534596 Page 20*; ;Source A, page 43 from *Alistair Cooke's America* ISBN-13: 978-0465018826 Penguin (Alistair Cooke) p.245, 2 Oct 2008, ; Source A, page 43 from *Hard Times: An Oral History of the Great Depression Page 419* ISBN-13: 978-1565846562, The New Press (Studs Terkel) 1 Jan 2001, with permission; Source B, page 48 adapted from *The American Dole: Unemployment Relief and the Welfare State in the Great Depression (Contributions in American History)* ISBN-13: 978-0313314001 Greenwood Press (Jeff Singleton) 30 Sep 2000, The American dole : unemployment relief and the welfare state in the Great Depression by SINGLETON, JEFF Reproduced with permission of GREENWOOD PUBLISHING GROUP in the format Republish in a book via Copyright Clearance Center. ; Source C, page 50 from *New Republic* (Edmund Wilson), February 1933 http://www.newrepublic.com; Extract Source E .37 from http://nationalheritagemuseum.org/Exhibitions/CurrentExhibitions/TeenageHoboesintheGreatDepression.aspx, Scottish Rite Masonic Museum and Library, Lexington, Massachusetts; Source F, page 52 from *Dust Bowl Diary* ISBN-13: 978-0803279131 University of Nebraska Press (Anne Marie Low) 1 Jun 1984; Source G, page 52 from *Dust Bowl: The Southern Plains in the 1930s* ISBN-13: 978-0195174885 *p11.* OUP USA (Donald Worster) 16 Sep 2004, With permission of Oxford University Press; Source A, page 60 from *Franklin D.Roosevelt and the New Deal (Historical Association pamphlets)* ISBN-13: 978-0852782125, The Historical Association (D K Adams) Jun 1979; Exhibit Source D .44 fromhttp://www.britannica.com/EBchecked/topic/405302/National-Recovery-Administration-NRA, Encyclopædia Britannica, Inc, Reprinted with permission from Encyclopaedia Britannica, © 2013 by Encyclopaedia Britannica, Inc.; Source D, page 67 from *Hard Times* ISBN-13: 978-1595587039, THE NEW PRESS (Studs Terkel) p.393, 15 Nov 2012, with permission;

In some instances we have been unable to trace the owners of copyright material, and we would appreciate any information that would enable us to do so.

A note from the publisher
In order to ensure that this student book offers high-quality support for the associated Edexcel qualification, it has been through a review process by the awarding organisation to confirm that it fully covers the teaching and learning content of the specification or part of a specification at which it is aimed, and demonstrates an appropriate balance between the development of subject skills, knowledge and understanding, in addition to preparation for assessment.

While the publishers have made every attempt to ensure that advice on the qualification and its assessment is accurate, the official specification and associated assessment guidance materials are the only authoritative source of information and should always be referred to for definitive guidance.

Edexcel examiners have not contributed to any updated sections in this resource relevant to examination papers for which they have responsibility.

No material from an endorsed student book will be used verbatim in any assessment set by Edexcel.

Endorsement of a student book does not mean that the student book is required to achieve this Edexcel qualification, nor does it mean that it is the only suitable material available to support the qualification, and any resource lists produced by the awarding organisation shall include this and other appropriate resources.